PORTRAIT OF
A COMMUNITY

Portrait of
a Community

The History and Roots of Homestead Heritage

A Brief Survey

by Blair Adams

Colloquium Press
Elm Mott, Texas

ISBN 978-0-916387-00-6

Published by

Colloquium Press
info@colloquiumpress.com

Printed in the United States of America

CONTENTS

ILLUSTRATIONS

GENERAL DESCRIPTION

Homestead Heritage is an agrarian- and craft-based intentional Christian community. Its literature stresses simplicity, sustainability, self-sufficiency, cooperation, service and quality craftsmanship. According to its neighbors, it also strives to live in peaceful coexistence with the land, other people and other faiths. On around 500 acres in central Texas, the community farms with draft animals and raises its own staple crops. These include wheat, oats, corn, potatoes, sweet potatoes, sweet sorghum, pinto beans and a cornucopia of fruits and vegetables. It mills its own grains in the community's water-wheel-run

gristmill, which is housed in a historic 250-year-old, hand-hewn, timber-framed mill. It holds an annual sorghum festival, harvesting cane and processing it into sweet syrup through its mule-driven sorghum mill. Whatever farm- or ranch-raised produce the community itself doesn't use is sold through the gristmill, through the community's restaurant, through its market or else is given away.

Homestead is internationally known for its quality craftsmanship. The community has a pottery house, a blacksmith shop, a leather-craft house, a cheese-making house, a woodworking and fine furniture-making shop, and a fiber-crafts cottage that features spinning, knitting and weaving. These shops are run by award-winning craftsmen and open year-round to the public. Homestead furniture makers have won top awards across the country and, by Presidential request, contributed fine pieces to the permanent White House Collection. Their work has been featured in numerous national publications.

Many other Homestead crafts are sold in their annual Homestead Fair at Thanksgiving, an event most recently attended by nearly 20,000 people. At least 30,000 others tour Homestead throughout the remainder of the year. In addition, the community hosts 3,000 to 5,000 public- and private-school children on tours every year. Many college classes also come out for seminars. Events at the Thanksgiving Fair include dozens of hands-on crafts for children, as well as demonstrations of barn raising, sheepdog events, horse farming, hand milking, pottery making, blacksmithing, woodworking, boat building, quilting,

weaving, spinning, basket making, boot making, cheese making, bread making and food preservation. (The community's artisan cheeses have won awards at international cheese shows, and its cheese makers provide products for fine restaurants across the state of Texas.) Seminars are also offered on homesteading and self-sufficiency skills. The community's 100-voice choir, as well as several children's choirs, sing for crowds of thousands, accompanied by their 40-piece orchestra. Several well-known musicians play instruments handcrafted by community members. In addition to the thousands of craft items sold at

the Fair, a wide array of multicultural dishes are offered in the Fair food booths (the community's restaurant has been written up in the *New York Times, Texas Monthly* and other periodicals). The highest quality crafts, which either journeymen or master craftsmen create, are sold year-round in the eighteenth-century barn that the community restored and erected in their craft village.

Homestead, in fact, restores more old American barns all across the country than probably anyone else. The historic barns have been saved from demolition by community craftsmen who carefully dismantle them and then transport the barns' great timber frames from and to locations coast to coast, finally reerecting them as elegant buildings for domestic, recreational and other purposes. Restored barns from Homestead can be found as far away as Japan. Numerous

restored eighteenth- and nineteenth-century historic structures also serve the community's own needs as seminar rooms, a weaving and spinning workshop, a retail craft store, a gristmill, as well as cheese making, bread making and food preservation classrooms. Another community craft service, Homestead Builders, has built homes for many prominent citizens,

including the President of the United States. The community has developed additional skills in building energy-efficient and off-the-grid housing. It also runs a general store that sells nearly everything needed to run a homestead—from how-to books to implements, seed, feed, hardware, pots, pans and just about anything else a homesteader might require.

In addition, the community runs the Ploughshare Institute for Sustainable Culture, which conducts year-round courses in all the above crafts and skills. These courses—such as woodworking, blacksmithing, pottery, spinning and weaving— take place in a setting much like that of a preindustrial village, where the craft shops are carefully configured into the natural surroundings. The Ploughshare also teaches many courses in homesteading skills, from gardening and canning to milking, cheese making and horse farming. These skills were first mastered on the community's own family-run homesteads. Although Homestead engages in many activities as a community (such as haying, corn harvest, sweet potato harvest, grain harvests and the like), the integrity of the family has always been stressed. So each family manages its own individual homestead.

Homestead, above and beyond the expenses of its other activities, has contributed millions of dollars to support single-parent households. Neither do any community members receive government welfare assistance. The community has also taught woodworking and other craft skills to those unable to afford such courses. And it has set up viable craft businesses for communities in third-world countries, also teaching them the agricultural skills necessary to sustain themselves independently and with dignity.

Homestead has received media coverage from many newspapers, as well as from both national and regional magazines and from television stations coast to coast. Almost all of the coverage has been exceedingly favorable.*

---

* Homestead has, however, also been the subject of one controversial newspaper story. That story was sponsored by a belief-surveillance group (a group whose representatives never visited the community nor ever attempted to contact even one of its members, except for one anonymous call in the middle of the night to threaten the community with its destruction). This surveillance group fed the paper comments solicited from select witnesses by using recovered-memory techniques (both suggestion and association). Moreover, the witnesses were all hostile to Homestead's Anabaptist belief system and favorable to the surveillance group's fundamentalist position. But area people rallied to Homestead's support, and visitors to Homestead more than doubled in the two years after the article. The same favorable results for the community occurred after a similarly based television program had used only people with a long record of determined hostility accompanied by repeated threats to destroy the community.

HOMESTEAD'S HISTORY

Homestead's beginnings go back to June of 1973, when Blair and Regina Adams moved into the Hell's Kitchen area of Manhattan's Lower East Side (he was 29; she was 21 and five months pregnant with their first baby). There, they rented an undersized cold-water flat and started a small peace church in what had formerly been

the Inferno Discotheque's bar and a crash pad for substance abusers and other down-and-out street people. People of many backgrounds—South American, Puerto Rican, African American, Jewish, Italian, German, Polish, Russian—began attending the meetings. Soon a small cluster of believers found themselves easing out of what they increasingly saw as the competitive frenzy of urban squalor and squander that surrounded them in New York City. Instead, they began to dedicate themselves to cooperating with and helping each other. Before long, they realized that, although they all still lived in their separate slum tenements, they nonetheless had almost inadvertently become a community—if of nothing else, then of heart and mind, of values and ideals, of hopes and dreams.

They immediately saw the need to impart to their children the cooperative values they themselves were learning. They knew that this would not be possible without shifting to a different kind of education. The educational model that had produced the pervasively competitive and specialized culture seemed destined to produce only more of the same. So they extensively studied education from every angle they could find, always seeking something that emphasized the wholeness of life. Their search reinforced a growing conviction that education would have to somehow be de-industrialized. Otherwise, they didn't see how they could ever achieve the results and the life they sought, or sustain such results if they were achieved. So, first, they set about to educate their children themselves and in their own homes. Then, later, they began to put together their own curriculum. They were aided in this when they were joined by many former public school teachers, even public school administrators and a former school superintendent—all of whom had come to similar conclusions about public education.

Their move toward home education in the 1970's preceded by a good number of years what became the now well-known movement across the country. So in pioneering into such uncharted territory, the community faced many challenges. One challenge even took them to court. There, they successfully defended the right of parents to direct the education of their children. The originally hostile judge finally even remarked that their program was the finest opportunity for children that he had ever seen. Since that time, they watched with disappointment as the home-school movement seemed to lose its original vision and goals. Instead, it more and more compromised itself until it increasingly became merely another component of the culture war, a war waged in a context where people competed economically, politically and socially, but where human life was increasingly desacralized and fragmented, losing the wholeness that characterizes all life. Yet Homestead continued pressing on in its own original goals.

Over time, they realized that each step they were taking, not just in schooling but in all areas of life, was forming a piece of a mosaic, and that a larger picture of an entirely different cultural alternative was emerging. Of course, they knew all along that they couldn't simply leap out of one culture and into another, but they believed they could keep taking discrete steps, one at a time.

So, after they started teaching their children, they next began seeking out patches of ground in the New York metropolitan area where they could grow at least a little of their own food. This, too, occurred in the 1970's. These efforts focused their attention across the Hudson River, in New Jersey. They began to see more and more how the way they had lived had actually cut them off from fully and directly participating in all those activities that were essential to human life. This included matters as simple but as absolutely necessary as eating; but it also included

other activities of the heart and mind, like teaching their own children. And, in that sense, they found that their old lifestyle had, ironically, cut them off from living. So they now eagerly thrust their hands into the soil, and even talked about how rich and good simple dirt smelled. Members continued to teach their own children and came to know the rewards of watching them learn and learning with them. They also began to give birth to their babies at home. They saw that birth was not a pathology that belonged in a hospital but the beginning of life that should begin in the place that best nurtured life—the self-sustaining home. More and more, they just wanted to live, *really* live. And when their elderly died of having fully lived, their children and grandchildren didn't want to give death the final victory by running from it—they wanted to overcome it with what had always held their lives together and given them meaning and purpose: self-sacrificing love. So they took care of their elderly and disabled, too, cherishing the opportunity to learn from the accumulated wisdom of a long life and to serve those who now fought to continue overcoming with love the most trying of life's circumstances, the greatest of its battles.

Each new level of participation brought unforeseen changes in their thinking, their feelings, their attitudes about life. So their relationships with each other, with creation and with God began to change, too. It came to them slowly that they were on a journey, not just back to their Anabaptist roots but back to life, a journey back down to earth with their bodies and back up to heaven with their souls. As all the pieces fell into place and the whole began to emerge, they felt life expanding in every direction—in breadth, depth, height and width—until a fully formed body of people, a community that could carry all that was essential to life, was finally being formed. They often described all that was changing in their lives as their "journey home."

But such journeys had always first demanded an exodus from one land before a people could find another. Soon, gardens weren't enough—they wanted to expand this realm of wholeness they had discovered, this realm of their new-found freedom to live. So they began to look for a larger piece of land and ended up in Colorado. By now, they were a hundred closely knit people. So a hundred people began to sell extraneous items, pack up the remaining meager possessions to prepare for the next great trek. They found temporary, make-do rental housing (mainly quadruplexes) in a mid-sized town in Colorado. Then they obtained their commercial licenses, rented huge 18-wheeler diesel trucks and began moving in August of 1979. To pay for the trips back and forth from the east coast to Colorado, they sold everything not essential to their new life. They would then haul out to Colorado a truckload of what was essential, next pick up onions in Oregon or potatoes in Idaho and finally haul them to Boston (they joked that, like the children of Israel, they figuratively had to "plunder Egypt" in order to escape it).

It took them six months to move everyone, since it took time to secure sufficient housing and to set up businesses. In every way, moving west was a new experience for these easterners. The roots of many went back generations in the New York metropolitan area—for some, this went back to the time when their families had first immigrated from the Old World. So when they went west, it was a new world to them, just as the east coast had been for their ancestors. One brother had never seen a tumbleweed, so he stopped, picked up the first one he saw, boxed it and sent it home to his mother.

The community couldn't buy land at first, so they rented a ten-acre farm and bought their first chickens, ducks, geese, sheep and draft horses. They decided to try to begin learning the rudiments of farming on a small scale until they could buy their own land.

Their service and construction businesses prospered, and in a few years they purchased a 700-acre farm with a year-round stream running through it. It was over 8 miles from the closest town, which was small, not much more than a village. So they felt more isolated from other people than they had wanted to be. But in one way, this probably ended up being for the best, since it gave them the opportunity to learn to farm without having to sacrifice so much time for a constant stream of visitors (though already many people from all over the world were visiting their farm). And, as it turned out, they needed a lot more time to learn how to farm than they had anticipated (when they left the East Coast megalopolis, one sister had thought corn ears

grew underground). And then it took even more time to learn how to farm with horses. Their training of draft animals at first only yielded broken thumbs, broken legs and broken farm implements but still unbroken horses. But they never really wanted to "break" horses—their goal was, less dramatically, to "gentle" them. Soon, they succeeded in the horse farming and were planting gardens, vineyards, potatoes, oats, flax and alfalfa. After they had mastered the basics, they were ready to move on and try to share their life with others.

So now they looked for a place closer to more people. Another fellowship had started in Texas, and then a Baptist church offered to give them a church building, the first they'd ever owned in all

those years. They moved to central Texas, bought land near Elm Mott (centrally located between Austin and Dallas), sold their farm in Colorado and started anew. There were some rough spots at first—a few people unfamiliar with the community confused them with David Koresh's notorious group in Waco, a group that hit the headlines at the same time that Homestead was just settling in. But before the tragic finale of this group had occurred, the Homestead community had already celebrated their first Fairs in Texas, and the local television station had done an especially favorable program on Homestead. Now, during the ensuing crisis, television stations swept in from Dallas, Houston and all over central Texas to help make clear

that, as one reporter stated, this "isn't the same group," that the two were "as different as night and day." The locals and many newspapers rallied once again to their support, and things soon settled down. All the while, they kept working, until finally everything described in the general description above had become a reality.

Whenever they stopped to take a breather and look around, they marveled at what had come to pass, at how far they had come from their old New York days on East 14th Street, in the slums of Hell's Kitchen. It all seemed like a dream, and people who had known them longest would even tell one of their oldest members, "I don't know anyone whose dreams have come true like yours." And they knew it was so. But they also knew that they were Anabaptists, and that the entire history of perhaps the most nonviolent people on earth had been one of suffering violence from other people's dislike of the unlike. So, while they rejoiced and thanked God for their many blessings, they also kept a close eye on the horizon, watching for any sign of mounting thunderheads. They knew that those who tried to climb to higher ground always brought themselves in reach of lightning bolts. But they continued to search out their roots and the ways of self-sacrificing love.

Historical Roots

The roots of Homestead Heritage's beliefs go back at least 500 years to the early sixteenth-century Anabaptist movement, which included the Mennonites, Amish and Brethren. The word *Anabaptist* was originally a derogatory byname applied by those who hated them. It means "re-baptizer" and actually carries far greater political, social and cultural implications for Western history than the seemingly innocuous and dull theological word might at first suggest.[1]

The history of this is important for those interested in knowing how the Western world came to institutionalize freedom and the separation of church and State. To begin with, the Anabaptists have probably held to a consistently nonviolent position longer than any other group of people in the world, and have done so in the face of great opposition. As a whole, they've walked in peace with their neighbors for half a millennium.[2] Their position on this emerged from long-standing struggles over an issue that proved central both to the church and to the secular world. The issue, in fact, came to dominate almost all of the West's culture wars, dating from the second century all the way into the twenty-first century.

The issue revolves around the question of whether or not the government will run the church or the church will run the government. The Anabaptists held that the only safe answer for everyone is, "neither." Based on Jesus' words to "render unto Caesar the things that are Caesar's and unto God the things that are God's," the Anabaptists believed in two separate spheres of polity and conscience that should not cross over into each other's territory. This, along with their determined position on nonviolence, set them at odds not only with both the Roman Catholic Church and the magisterial Protestant Reformers like Zwingli, Calvin and Luther, but also with the ostensibly

secular political authorities that became so closely tied to these other churches.[3] This latter group of secular leaders found it, at the time, convenient to conscript people's religious passions to serve the ruler's own political cause, although such passions were presumably supposed to be directed wholly toward God. The Hapsburg emperors had long followed this course with Catholicism, and now the emerging secular leaders

of Germany's some 300-odd principalities seized upon the newly developing Protestant passions, using them to help pry these principalities loose from the political grip of Charles V, the Catholic emperor of the Hapsburg Empire at the time.[4]

The Hapsburg dynasty, following the example of Charlemagne, had explicitly modeled itself after the Roman emperor Constantine the Great.[5] So it is not surprising that the emperor, devout as he may have been, would nonetheless depend on the Catholic Church to provide the *political* unity and hegemony his empire required. But the princes and rulers of the small kingdoms and territories within Charles's vast domain chafed under the emperor's political yoke. They wanted to shake off his restraints upon their own desires for expanded territory, independence and power. They therefore welcomed the chance to use the rising Protestant sects to build territorial support in their struggles against the emperor. This politicization of religion later led to the Thirty Years' War, which historian Peter Wilson has shown was primarily a political struggle that merely *used* religion, rather than a religious war that used politics.[6] Indeed, depending on political advantage, principalities and even whole kingdoms

switched allegiance from Catholic to Protestant, from Protestant to Catholic, and then back again.[7] Thus staunchly Catholic France

joined in an alliance with Lutheran Sweden and Calvinist Holland against both Catholic Spain and the Catholic Hapsburg emperor.[8] And the army of these latter Catholic powers was one-third Protestant! Also, Lutheran Sweden fought Lutheran Denmark.[9] Neither did Saxony, Brandenburg and other principalities hesitate to switch sides if they could gain political advantage.[10] Similarly, Presbyterian Scots fought for Catholic France and Poland, as well as for the Catholic emperor, while many Gaelic Catholics fought for Protestant Denmark, Holland and Sweden.[11] The fact that so many men converted back and forth, in accord with whichever political ruler they fought under, shows just which allegiance— religious or political—took precedence and proved most decisive. Many such anomalies testified to the fact that, as Wilson's standard history on the subject shows, this was not primarily a religious struggle. So the infamous "wars of religion" were not, ironically, primarily about religion but about political power. Yet these wars were then, even more ironically, used to consolidate the very political power that had just torn Europe apart.

There were, of course, princes who felt natural affinities for the emerging Protestant sects, but none of these religious affinities trumped the political advantages that might be gained by shifting

allegiance from Catholicism to one of the new and popular faiths, or to switch back again.[12] At least this was true of the vast majority of territorial rulers, with perhaps only one or two notable exceptions. And the Anabaptists, determined as they were to avoid *all* political alliances, but nonetheless seeing that religion was on every hand prostituting itself to political designs, desperately scrambled to find refuge under such exceptional rulers.[13]

It was not easy, however, to seek refuge in a principality and at the same time effectively resist the pressures from the prince to form a political entanglement or to avoid fighting in the prince's army—after all, such a relationship had been a feudal tradition for over a thousand years. So the Anabaptists soon discovered that not only were the Catholic authorities seeking to snuff them out, but also that the emerging magisterial Reformers—Reformers who had found common cause with the civil magistracies and secular governments of their respective territories—wanted to use those governments to gain territorial religious monopolies by eliminating all competing faiths, with a special emphasis on destroying the Anabaptists.

In short, both Catholics and magisterial Reformers wanted to coerce human conscience and force everyone in their respective territories to conform their beliefs to those of the religious leaders who had been endorsed by the secular rulers. Apparently, even the newly emerging magisterial Reformers did not see truth as sufficiently compelling in itself to inspire

people to freely embrace it—instead, the Reformers joined many Catholics in believing people had to be externally compelled to accept truth, or at least to conform to the dictates of those who had taken it upon themselves to police everyone's beliefs. This position would be made the official policy of Europe in the treaty known as the Peace of Augsburg, which established the principle of *cuius regio, eius religio*: the ruler's religion determines the subject's religion.[14]

As in so many other ways concerning issues that still very much affect people's lives today, Martin Luther played a paradoxical role in setting the stage for the unfolding drama. At the beginning of the Reformation, Luther had spoken of the need for a church in which believers "who wanted to be

Christians in earnest and who professed the gospel with hand and mouth" would voluntarily "sign their names" in a form of written covenant commitment and "meet alone in a house somewhere to pray, to read, to baptize . . . and do other Christian works."[15] Such a vision of the church excluded any interference from the coercive power of the State to either force people to enter the church or to compel them to conform their views to a governmentally enforced orthodoxy. Within the setting that Luther originally proposed, the only discipline would be based on the mutual agreement to voluntarily maintain the conditions to which members had originally agreed. In this small group setting, those who did not truly "lead Christian lives could be known, reproved, corrected [or] cast out . . . according to the rule of Christ, Matthew 18:15-17."[16] The goal of such a policy was not to compel belief on unwilling subjects but to maintain viability as an alternative community composed of individuals freely committed, in Luther's words, to "centering everything on the Word, prayer and love."[17]

But according to Yale's Roland Bainton, Luther faced a dilemma: "He wanted both a confessional church based on personal faith and experience" and "a territorial church" that would include everyone "in a given locality." As Bainton noted, "If [Luther] were forced to choose, he would take his stand with the masses"—that is, with the territorial church whose beliefs *everyone* would have to accept; "and this was the direction" that Luther finally took, dropping his original ideal of uncoerced and voluntary commitment.[18]

Luther's decision to focus his attention on establishing "a territorial church," however, rested in large part on the fact that he never broke free from the notion that had slipped into the church centuries before, under Constantine, and which only seemed to have reached a certain level of culmination during the reign of the emperor Theodosius in 380 A.D. This was the notion that the voluntary, noncoercive authority of the church (a kingdom "*not* of this world") could somehow marry the compulsory, political power (a kingdom "*of* this world") and thus form a State-church, an oxymoronic "Christian nation."[19]

Luther's confusion of these two radically different types of authority destroyed his initial hope of "Christians who earnestly love the Word finding each other and joining together."[20] Instead, as Professor Durnbaugh documented, Luther opted "to turn to the prince in order to get on with the task of securing the Reformation" against his Catholic and Anabaptist adversaries.[21] Because of this decision, "Protestantism" in part issued forth in "tragedy," for "when . . . groups did emerge in history" displaying the very voluntary, noncoercive qualities of the believers' church that Luther had originally desired— namely, the Anabaptists—"Luther and his colleagues could see nothing in them but enthusiasts, fanatics and rebels."[22] So he sought to crush them through the exercise of external State compulsion. Eventually, Luther went so far as to declare that those attending voluntary, free assemblies of believers, believers that stood outside State-church regulation, were "scamps" whom "the magistrate [should] consign . . . into the hands of [their] proper master—whose name is Meister Hans," that is, "the hangman."[23]

So the Anabaptists became the one group that everyone—Catholics, magisterial Reformers and most of the secular authorities who were aligned with both—could agree to target.[24] Everyone agreed, that is, that the Anabaptists should simply be wiped out. Some said the Anabaptists deserved this fate because of their determined refusal to admit any need for violence or for reliance on any civil power in order to establish the church. But the Anabaptists insisted that the day the church first took such a course, joining hand in hand with Constantine, marked precisely the point of derailment from the path that Jesus had proclaimed when He spoke of the coming of a "kingdom *not* of this world," a kingdom where people "turned the other cheek," "loved their enemies" and "returned good for evil." The Anabaptists called this tragic shift in courses the "Constantinian synthesis."[25] It was, in their view, the time when State and church fused as one, when the brute coercive authority of Caesar merged with the gentle noncoercive authority of Christ to produce a monstrous hybrid, the skeletal visage of the angel of death arrayed in bridal garments, swinging a sickle and riding the beast of Statism to ravage the earth in the name of the love of Christ. This was merely "Santa Muerte," "holy death," now resurrected in its modern form as a secularized civil religion.

The Anabaptists wanted no part of it, even if for them it meant suffering and death. They saw this suffering as the path that Christ had chosen—to suffer and die rather than capitulate to the forces of suffering and death by resorting to their powers in self-defense. So they rejected any reliance on the power of death, either to defend themselves or to triumph temporarily over their enemies. Instead, they said they would rely on the power of life, which their Scriptures described as constituting God's very nature—love. And, after all, they added, hadn't Peter told Christians that they were called to such a path?[26] All this explains why Roger Olson, theologian of church history at Baylor University, called the Anabaptists "the heroes of the Reformation." They were the only ones, Olson said, who "did not persecute" anyone else.[27]

Their enemies, however, couldn't have been happier with their position—it made the defenseless Anabaptists seem so easy to exterminate. And yet, after 500 years, they still remain a small but important religious presence in the world today. More significantly, many nations (and denominations), after

several hundred years, would eventually adopt their position by separating church and State, although what has been left to the noncoercive authority of Christ's love seems to the Anabaptists to have shrunk to a private sphere so small as to have become all but nonexistent in the face of increasingly totalitarian States, States that ironically often arose as "Christian Nations," just as had the Lutheran Germany that turned into the millennial nightmare of the Nazi *Führerstaat*.

In the early days of the Anabaptists, given their favorable reputation among the neighbors they were so willing to help in times of crisis or need, the only difficulty their enemies had in trying to destroy them was in finding a way to undermine their generally good reputation. The way to do this handily presented itself in the uprising at the city of Munster in Westphalia during the years 1534-35.[28] There, two followers of Melchior Hoffman, one, a man named Jan Matthys (a baker from Haarlem) and a second man named John of Leiden (a tailor), proclaimed Munster to be the "New Jerusalem," which they said would now usher in the millennial kingdom.[29] Apparently this would happen through polygamy (John of Leiden took 16 wives), beheadings (against unruly wives) and violence against secular authorities.[30] In short, these maverick men were the David Koreshes of their day.

In the meantime, Munster's expelled bishop, Franz von Waldeck besieged the town, killing Matthys, parading his head on a pole and nailing his privates to the city gates. John of Leiden immediately took over, proclaiming himself King David's successor and king of Munster.[31] By Easter, the city had fallen, its wild leaders tortured and executed. Their corpses rotted in three cages hanging from the steeple of St. Lambert's Church, where the cages still hang today.[32] All the enemies of the emerging Anabaptists could not resist the sudden inspiration to engage in a little religious opportunism by quickly labeling those of the Munster rebellion, "Anabaptists." The only problem was that they weren't—at least, the Munsterites shared little or nothing in common with the nonviolent groups that the Catholics and magisterial Reformers had, in fact, been targeting as Anabaptists.[33]

Actually, the main body of Anabaptists—the Swiss Brethren and the followers of Menno Simons (1496-1561)—had less in common with the Munster radicals than did others who called themselves Christians. The Munster radicals even had more in common with magisterial Reformers like John Calvin or Martin Luther in one crucial way: the Munsterites didn't hesitate to resort to violence. And, just like the Munsterites, Calvin, for

instance, had taken the physician, Michael Servetus, the discoverer of the pulmonary system, and burned him at the stake simply because the latter wouldn't confess to what Calvin thought was the proper doctrine of the trinity.[34] And Luther didn't hesitate to recommend eliminating the hapless and suffering peasants in the Peasants' Revolt of 1524 or to consign the Anabaptists to the hangman. Whereas in contrast, Anabaptist Conrad Grebel (1498-1526), known as "the Father of Anabaptism," had, early on, written a letter reproving Thomas Müntzer for his violence.*[35] Anabaptists Dirk Philips and Menno Simons had later done the same with the Munster rebels.[36]

---

* Müntzer, who led one segment of the Peasants' Revolt ten years prior to the Munster Rebellion, was also falsely, but conveniently, associated with the Anabaptist movement by some.

But to make these distinctions between two widely divergent groups among radical Reformers didn't serve the agendas of either Catholics or magisterial Reformers, who both seemed adrift in an early form of Korsakoff's syndrome. Both Catholic and Protestant leaders knew, however, that Anabaptists like Grebel and Simons radically differed from violent aberrations like Thomas Müntzer, Jan Matthys and John of Leiden. But, given the open commitment of the State churches to coercing

human conscience, they could not forgo so perfect a chance to smear as wild and violent killers all those irritating dissidents they could now lump together and dispose of under the label of "Anabaptists." By doing so, they could use guilt-by-association to set up for elimination an otherwise well-liked and respected religious group, a group that had proven difficult to destroy by merely accusing them of holding allegedly incorrect doctrines. At the same time, this maneuver allowed the State churches to forgo the onerous task of engaging in an open forum about what exactly did constitute Biblical truth. It was much easier to simply use State-backed oppression to trump the call for open dialogue, especially when such oppression would be publicly approved now that the target had been not merely maligned through occasional misrepresentation but also had now been saturated in the hydrocarbons of partial truths and outright lies. Only the right spark was needed to ignite the fuel of this rabid intolerance.

It was not the first time confabulation was used to set someone up for the flames, and it would not be the last. This method had already been used with great effect against the Jewish community: aberrant examples were put forth as typically Jewish; and the lie was then constantly repeated until everyone automatically imposed upon the whole Jewish community the ugly template derived from fear-mongering propaganda. Then the testimony of a few choice ex-members of the Jewish community, often eccentric ex-members with vendettas and well-known to be on the make, could be selectively solicited to confirm what propaganda had made a common prejudice of the time—that innocent Jews were exactly what their most vicious enemies had always tried to make them out to be: social pathogens. So now, with the Anabaptists, the slaughter would begin anew.

Centuries of Persecution

Probably few other Christian groups have suffered so many years of such consistent and vicious persecution as have the Anabaptists. Yale's Bainton and others have shown that their relentless adversaries exterminated virtually every Anabaptist leader in Germany.[37] Renowned Holocaust scholar, Frank Littell, even stated that if this nonviolent strain of Christianity had been preserved instead of targeted for extermination, the Nazi Holocaust might never have occurred, for there would have remained a vital German tradition of resistance to tyrannical State authority.[38] It appears, however, that their own nonviolence made the Anabaptists seem more vulnerable to religious bullies on every European block.

Defenselessness, it appears, provoked greater aggressiveness, brutality and even blood lust—surprisingly, this aggressiveness came mostly from among other professing Christians, who used the secular State to do the messy work of eliminating any competition to their creeds. Yet through it all, the Anabaptist witness of nonviolence continued unabated.

The first Anabaptist martyr was probably 29-year-old Felix Manz (1498-1527). Manz believed only in a believer's baptism, specifically referring only to believers who had made a free choice, rather than to an infant who had no choice or to an adult forced to be baptized. Because of this belief in the freedom to choose, Manz, as the former "star pupil and protégé" of Zwingli

was sentenced, with Zwingli's approval, to death by drowning.[39] Both Catholics and magisterial Reformers saw drowning as the appropriate "third baptism" for all these "rebaptizers." So in the middle of Zurich, and in the dead of winter, Manz's feet were bound together, a stick was run behind his knees, his hands were lashed to the stick, and he was tossed unceremoniously into the Limmat River.[40]

Thousands of other Anabaptists were hunted down by the religious Gestapo of that day—the *Täuferjäger*. They were tortured, drowned or burned at the stake, many of them women and children. Those children not executed were taken from their parents and given to people who would reindoctrinate them

in a State-approved religion.[41] Yet the Anabaptists nonetheless persisted in their beliefs of nonviolence, as well as separation of church and State.[42]

Michael Sattler (1490-1527) was another respected Anabaptist leader. He was the author of the influential Schleitheim Confession, which stressed liberty of conscience.

For having "seduced pious people" with such damnable heresies as nonviolence, not swearing oaths and baptizing only adult believers who had freely chosen to be baptized, Sattler's tongue was cut out, and "red-hot tongs" were used five separate times to "tear pieces from his body." Then, still refusing to recant, "he was burned to ashes as a heretic."

His wife, too, was forcibly drowned a few days later.[43] Merely to be married to Sattler apparently sufficed as a crime warranting the death penalty.

Other prominent leaders soon followed, like Balthasar Hubmaier (1481-1528). He had been one of the leading Catholic scholars in Europe, and at the age of 34 was appointed vice-rector at Germany's prestigious Ingolstadt University. Seven years later he became a Protestant, much to the chagrin of Catholics and to the glee of magisterial Reformers. The latter did not gloat long, however, since three years later Hubmaier began to teach against infant baptism and joined the Anabaptist Swiss Brethren. After a debate in Zurich,

Zwingli, piqued by his opponent's incisive arguments, had Hubmaier tortured, forcing a confession from him. Later, this Anabaptist leader (now solidly unrepentant of his "heresy") was burned at the stake. Three days afterward, his wife was forcibly drowned in the Danube River.[44] Again, even being the wife of an Anabaptist minister had become a capital offense.

Each successive generation of Anabaptists has struggled to believe those who so confidently and repeatedly have assured them that now times were different, that they had nothing more to fear, that such fears were foolish in such an enlightened place and era, an era that had forever put behind it intolerance and cruelty. Yet the reality has proven to far differ from either the claims or the hopes. In the era of the Enlightenment in the 1700's, many Amish, Mennonites, Hutterites and Dunkers had fled to America under severe persecution in Europe.[45] Yet in America, too, their deeply held convictions against violence soon brought the torch of persecution once again to bear against their peace-loving beliefs. Professor Carl Bowman writes that at the outbreak of the Revolutionary War "those who refused to enroll in the militia" because of their nonviolent beliefs "faced heavy fines, public embarrassment and acts of vandalism. Some were compelled to furnish money and goods to families who had suffered from the conflict, and others to provide horses, wagons, and supplies to military installations. Lists were prepared and sometimes publicly posted of those who refused to enroll. These . . . included Brethren, Mennonites, and others whose faith prevented them from fighting. The posture of Christian nonparticipation in the rebellion was one for which a pro-revolutionary public had little sympathy."[46]

According to historians, this unsympathetic public was "suspicious of the Dunkers" and other Anabaptists for not fighting, dying or killing and "wanted to see" them "punished." The most "devastating penalty ever exacted of a Brethren was handed down in Frederick, Maryland, on July 6, 1781." It was against a "Dunker by the name of Peter Suman, along with two others." Here is how the grim sentence reads: "You shall be carried to the jail of Frederick county and thence be drawn to the gallows of Frederick-town and be hanged thereon—You shall be cut down to the earth alive and your bowels shall be taken out and burnt, while you are yet alive, [and] your heads shall be cut off, your bodies shall be divided into four parts, and your heads and quarters shall be placed where his excellency the governor shall appoint." So the "mutilated bodies [of the slain] were carted about the town and nailed up on posts for public display; . . . some parts decayed and were fed to the dogs; . . . Suman's widow and friends removed parts of his body under cover of darkness in order to bury them."[47]

An example of another such "traitor" was a "Germantown printer and Dunker elder [and pioneer], Christopher Sauer II. After returning home from British-held Philadelphia in May of 1778, he was taken prisoner by rebel forces and marched at bayonet point to Valley Forge, where he was held for five days.

Denied permission to return to Germantown until late July (for refusing to swear allegiance to the American cause [the Anabaptists would not swear oaths of *any* kind for anyone]), he was denounced as a traitor in his absence and returned home only to have his personal possessions confiscated and auctioned off . . . . Left with next to nothing, he was quickly aided by the Brethren."[48] He remained a Brethren minister for the next three years until his death, a death largely due to the ordeal he had suffered. He had, however, taken pains during his final days to repay the money that had been loaned to him by his spiritual brothers.[49]

Even in spite of such incidents, conditions in America were, in general, incomparably more favorable than in Europe.

Therefore many waves of persecuted refugees continued to flock to American shores. Some had early on instead fled Germany for Russia, only to then be forced to flee Russia under Bolshevik persecution in what was called "the Great Trek." These also finally made their way to North America, carrying the wheat seed they had developed for the Russian climate (we call it "Turkey Red") to the northern United States and Canada, an area that soon became the world's breadbasket while Russia was left to now buy wheat from the United States.

But when World War I broke out, even those Anabaptists who had come to America in one of the earlier waves also realized

they still had not escaped the iron fist of persecution. One of many such stories vividly makes the point. The Hutterites in the United States numbered not quite two thousand when the nation entered World War I. These communal farmers, who had

fled persecution in Central Europe and Russia, had, by around
the turn of the century, transformed marginal, unused land into
a series of small, peaceful and law-abiding religious colonies,
primarily in the Dakotas. The Brethren, too, felt constrained
from any participation in the military, even simply wearing the
uniform or performing work supportive of the military. While
they willingly gave money to war relief efforts, they could not in
good conscience participate in any way in the war effort itself.[50]

Confrontation arose with mass conscription in 1917, for the
United States did not then allow conscientious objection to
all military service, only objection to combatant service. The
Brethren had agreed among themselves that Scripture required
their compliance with the law as far as possible. So they agreed
to register for the draft and report for physical examinations
but felt constrained from submitting to actual induction. As
the few dozen young Brethren men of draft age began arriving
at the draft centers, U.S. military "officers were determined to
pressure the men into military service by any means in their

power, psychological or physical. By means of argument or casual observations, they tried to detect inconsistencies in the Hutterite position . . . . At Camp Funston some of the men were brutally handled in the guardhouse. They were bayoneted, beaten and tortured by various forms of water 'cure.'"[51] But they continued to cling to their beliefs.

Jakob S. Waldner, who resisted induction at Camp Funston, kept an extensive diary of his experiences at the camp, experiences that John A. Hostetler notes "were common to all sincere conscientious objectors, including Mennonites and those of other religious faiths." Waldner recorded that he and others were "thrown fully clothed into a cold shower for twenty minutes for refusing a work order. After such cold showers, the men were often thrown out of a window and dragged along the ground by their hair and feet by soldiers who were waiting outside. Their beards were disfigured to make them appear ridiculous . . . . The Hutterite men resented the frequent physical examinations requiring them to appear nude for inspections for venereal disease . . . . One night, eighteen men were aroused from their sleep and held under cold showers until one of them

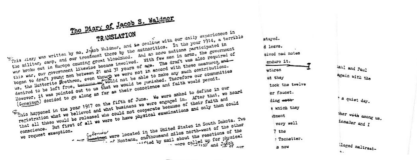

Camp Funston, Kan.

became hysterical. Others were hung by their feet [head first into] tanks of water until they almost choked to death. On many days they were made to stand at attention on the cold side of their barracks, in scant clothing, while those who passed by scoffed at them in abusive and foul language. They were chased across the fields by guards on motorcycles under the guise of taking exercise, until they dropped from sheer exhaustion."[52]

Upon receiving word of the events at the induction centers, the Hutterite elders urgently appealed to President Wilson and subsequently gained an appointment for an audience with the secretary of war. After traveling by train across country to

Washington, D.C., in a brief meeting with the secretary, the elders received only the curt advice that their children should report to their respective training centers and then do whatever their

conscieces would allow. No help was offered to resolve the conflict and the violent abuse.[53]

Shortly after this, four more young Hutterian men—Jacob Wipf and three Hofer brothers, Joseph, David and Michael— were summoned to Fort Lewis, Washington. They, like others before them, received the standard examinations and were then sent to the induction officers. Upon refusing induction, military officers placed the young men in the guardhouse, and a military

court subsequently sentenced them to thirty-seven years in prison. Four armed lieutenants handcuffed and chained them for their trip to the notorious Alcatraz prison. Once there, they were locked in "a 'dungeon' of darkness, filth and stench and put in solitary confinement out of earshot of each other."[54] Their guards hung army uniforms before each of them in their solitary

cells, telling each young man, now separated from all support, that only death could spare him from wearing the uniform, which, to the young men, symbolized allegiance to the violence of military conflict.[55]

A Johns Hopkins University publication describes the subsequent course of events: "For several days the young men slept on the cold, wet concrete floor wearing nothing but their light underwear. They received half a glass of water every twenty-four hours but no food. They were beaten with clubs and, with arms crossed, tied to the ceiling. After five days they were taken from the 'hole' for a short time. Their wrists

were so swollen from insect bites and skin eruptions that they could not put on their own jackets. For the remaining months at Alcatraz, they were allowed one hour of outdoor exercise each Sunday afternoon. After four months at Alcatraz the men were transferred to Fort Leavenworth, Kansas, by six armed sergeants." Jacob, Joseph, David and Michael "arrived at their destination at 11 P.M., after four days and five nights of travel, chained together two by two. From the railway station to the

military prison they were marched on foot through the streets and prodded with bayonets. Although they were handcuffed, they managed to carry their satchels in one hand and their Bibles in the other. On arrival at the prison, soaked with sweat, they were compelled to remove their outer clothing. Two hours later, when they received their prison clothing, they were chilled to the bone."[56]

The following morning as they stood in the cold, Joseph and Michael collapsed and had to be carried to the infirmary. Jacob and David went to solitary confinement and a starvation diet. In solitary, they "were made to stand nine hours each day with hands tied and their feet barely touching the floor."[57] Jacob had somehow managed to slip out a telegram to their wives back home in South Dakota, who immediately set out by train, along with a male attendant, to Fort Leavenworth. After a one-day delay caused by conflicting information from authorities as to

their husbands' whereabouts, finally "the women arrived at midnight [at Fort Leavenworth] to find their husbands nearly dead. When they returned in the morning, Joseph was dead. The guards refused his wife, Maria, permission to see the dead body. In tears, she pleaded with the colonel and was finally taken to the casket only to find that her husband's body had been dressed in the military uniform he had so adamantly refused to wear. Michael Hofer died two days later. The wives and a few other relatives accompanied the bodies to their home community, where their enormous funeral seared Hutterite minds with the price of true apostolic faith."[58] So even death had not spared Joseph from wearing the uniform, and before the war had ended, almost all the members of these communities had fled to Canada, at great sacrifice of property, peace of mind and life.

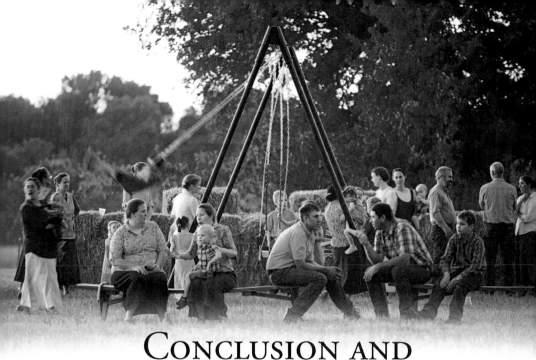

CONCLUSION AND
VIEWPOINT

From the days of the Constantinian synthesis on down to modern times, a steady stream of pogroms, inquisitions and "witch" trials has pockmarked the history of the Western world. Although formerly these aberrations of Christianity had only occurred under the auspices of a State-backed Roman Catholicism, now, with the coming of the magisterial Reformation, they also occurred in places like Zurich, Munich, Amsterdam, London and Salem—all under the aegis of Protestantism. But these attempts of the church to purge out any hint of nonconformity to what its learned councils dictated as the dogmas people would be allowed to believe have, tragically, ended in the slaughter of far more Jews, Anabaptists, Quakers and other dissident peace Christians than they ever did anyone who might have remotely resembled a witch. But always those policing the earth, in the name of Christ, of some political ideology or a combination of the two, ferreting out all unauthorized thoughts and beliefs, have only lent credence to the words of Jesus—that persecution arises most often from among those who are fully and obdurately convinced, as Michael Sattler's accusers expressly stated they were, that they were doing God (whether the Biblical God or merely their own apotheosized causes, minds, personalities, beliefs and polities) a service.[59]

Homestead Heritage has known what it means to have joined the long line of Anabaptists who have peacefully accepted persecution. Although the community has *fought* for the truth, it has never seen the attempt to gently refute lies as equivalent to hurting or destroying people. So it has also fought to maintain love toward not only their neighbors but also their enemies. Persecution has nonetheless come to the community, usually at the hands of many of the same sorts of religious antagonists who have always attacked the Anabaptists, and Homestead's attackers have also used much the same tactics and the same sort

of unreliable sources and witnesses. Homestead's property has been defaced with swastikas (it is well-known that it has many Jewish members), its pulpit desecrated by vandals, its children threatened in deranged letters and (in Colorado) even shot at as they gathered their milk cows. But the Homestead community has come to accept that all this is part of the Christian walk, and that, like Jesus, they must accept the world's bad along with God's good—believing that accepting *both* in nonresisting submission can serve the purpose of establishing the enduring rule of love in their own lives, and even perhaps in the lives of others. This is a position they have committed to strive for and maintain.

Through its entire history, peace has been central to all their efforts. One indication of some measure of their success occurred in the summer of 2010, when an Arab Christian from

Lebanon, an Arab Muslim from Bahrain and a Jewish Israeli Christian who lived at Homestead all got together at Homestead and sat down to talk. The conversation went on for hours. At the end, there was a deep feeling of peace and good will, and one of the Arabs said, "Isn't it amazing that we can all sit and talk like this in this place but that we couldn't do this in our own countries?"

Notes

1.   John A. Hostetler, *Hutterite Society* (Baltimore, Md.: Johns Hopkins University Press, 1974), p. 5; Roger E. Olson, *The Story of Christian Theology: Twenty Centuries of Tradition and Reform* (Downers Grove, Ill.: InterVarsity Press, 1999), pp. 393, 417.

2.   Erwin Fahlbusch and Geoffrey William Bromiley, *The Encyclopedia of Christianity*, vol. 4 (Grand Rapids, Mich.: Wm. B. Eerdmans, 2005), pp. 54-55.

3.   William R. Estep, *The Anabaptist Story* (Grand Rapids, Mich.: William B. Eerdmans Publishing Co., 1975), pp. 22, 43, 48-49; *The Mennonite Encyclopedia: A Comprehensive Reference Work on the Anabaptist-Mennonite Movement*, vol. 1 (Hillsboro, Kans.: Mennonite Brethren Publishing House, 1955), p. 498; Roland H. Bainton, *The Reformation of the Sixteenth Century* (Boston: Beacon Press, 1956), pp. 97, 102.

4.   Peter H. Wilson, *The Thirty Years War: Europe's Tragedy* (Cambridge, Mass.: Harvard University Press, Belknap Press, 2009), pp. 17, 24, 78-81, 99-102, 109-13; Donald Kagan, Steven Ozment and Frank M. Turner, *The Western Heritage*, 5th ed. (Englewood Cliffs, N.J.: Prentice Hall, 1995), p. 467.

5.   Wilson, *Thirty Years War*, pp. 19-20, 776.

6.   Wilson, *Thirty Years War*, pp. 9, 27-28.

7.   Wilson, *Thirty Years War*, pp. 35, 38-39, 60-61, 63, 550-51; William P. Guthrie, *The Later Thirty Years War: From the Battle of Wittstock to the Treaty of Westphalia* (Westport, Conn.: Greenwood Press, 2003), p. 6.

8.   Wilson, *Thirty Years War*, pp. 552, 555-57, 619.

9.   Wilson, *Thirty Years War*, p. 678.

10. Wilson, *Thirty Years War*, pp. 574-75, 628-29.

11. Wilson, *Thirty Years War*, p. 830; Tryntje Helfferich, ed. and trans., *The Thirty Years War: A Documentary History* (Indianapolis, Ind.: Hackett Publishing Co., 2009), pp. 113, 146, 314.

12. Wilson, *Thirty Years War*, pp. 58-64, 205-13, 223-24, 289, 830.

13. Estep, *Anabaptist Story*, pp. 3, 49, 100, 104, 125.

14. Donald F. Durnbaugh, *The Believers' Church: The History and Character of Radical Protestantism* (Scottdale, Pa.: Herald Press, 1985), p. 29.

15. Martin Luther, "The German Mass and Order of Service," in *Luther's Works*, vol. 53, *Liturgy and Hymns*, ed. Ulrich S. Leupold and Helmut T. Lehmann (Philadelphia: Fortress Press, 1965), p. 64.

16. Luther, "German Mass and Order of Service," p. 64.

17. Luther, "German Mass and Order of Service," p. 64.

18. Roland H. Bainton, *Here I Stand: A Life of Martin Luther* (New York: New American Library, A Mentor Book, 1950), p. 243.

19. J. Denny Weaver, "Renewing Theology: The Way of John Howard Yoder," *Fides et Historia,* Summer/Fall 2003, pp. 86-87.

20. Luther, "German Mass and Order of Service," p. 64.

21. Durnbaugh, *Believers' Church,* p. 4.

22. Durnbaugh, *Believers' Church,* p. 4.

23. Durnbaugh, *Believers' Church,* p. 233.

24. Estep, *Anabaptist Story,* pp. 9-10; Bainton, *Reformation of the Sixteenth Century,* pp. 101-102.

25. A. James Reimer, *Mennonites and Classical Theology: Dogmatic Foundations for Christian Ethics* (Kitchener, Ontario: Pandora Press, 2001), p. 259.

26. 1 Pet. 2:19-24; 3:8-18; 4:12-15.

27. Verbal communication between Blair Adams and Roger E. Olson, professor of Christian Theology and Ethics at George W. Truett Theological Seminary, Baylor University.

28. Leonard Verduin, *The Reformers and Their Stepchildren* (1964; reprint, Sarasota, Fla.: Christian Hymnary Publishers, 1991), p. 238; Owen Chadwick, *The Reformation* (New York: Penguin Books, 1972), pp. 190-91.

29. Chadwick, *The Reformation,* p. 190; Estep, *Anabaptist Story,* pp. 108-11.

30. Henry Chadwick and G. R. Evans, eds., *Atlas of the Christian Church* (New York: Facts on File, 1989), p. 102.

31. Chadwick, *The Reformation,* p. 190; Walter Klaassen, *Living at*

the End of the Ages: Apocalyptic Expectation in the Radical Reformation (Lanham, Md.: University Press of America, 1992), pp. 49-50; Estep, *Anabaptist Story*, p. 111.

32. Klaassen, *Living at the End of the Ages*, p. 50; Chadwick, *The Reformation*, p. 191.

33. Chadwick, *The Reformation*, p. 191; Roger L. Berry, *God's World— His Story* (Harrisonburg, Va.: Christian Light Publications, 1976), pp. 376-77.

34. Perez Zagorin, *How the Idea of Religious Toleration Came to the West* (Princeton, N.J.: Princeton University Press, 2003), pp. 93-95.

35. Verduin, *Reformers and Their Stepchildren*, p. 234; Conrad Grebel et al., "Letter to Thomas Müntzer (1524)," in *The Protestant Reformation*, ed. Hans J. Hillerbrand (New York: Harper and Row Publishers, 1969), p. 127.

36. Estep, *Anabaptist Story*, pp. 112-13; Verduin, *Reformers and Their Stepchildren*, pp. 237-38.

37. Bainton, *Reformation of the Sixteenth Century*, pp. 105, 107; Olson, *Story of Christian Theology*, p. 417; *Encyclopaedia Britannica Micropaedia*, 15th ed., s.v. "Anabaptists."

38. Verbal communication between Kevin Durkin, Colloquium Press, and Franklin H. Littell, professor emeritus at Temple University, 2 July 1991.

39. Olson, *Story of Christian Theology*, p. 417.

40. Olson, *Story of Christian Theology*, pp. 417, 393; Estep, *Anabaptist Story*, p. 32.

41. Olson, *Story of Christian Theology*, p. 417.

42. Bainton, *Reformation of the Sixteenth Century*, p. 102.

43. "The Trial and Martyrdom of Michael Sattler," in *The Protestant Reformation*, ed. Lewis W. Spitz (Englewood Cliffs, N.J.: Prentice-Hall, 1966), pp. 100-101; Bruce Gordon, *The Swiss Reformation* (New York: Manchester University Press, 2002), p. 202.

44. Olson, *Story of Christian Theology*, pp. 418-19.

45. Jeffrey D. Schultz, John G. West Jr. and Iain Maclean, eds., *Encyclopedia of Religion in American Politics* (Phoenix, Ariz.: Oryx Press, 1999), p. 15; David E. Shi, *In Search of the Simple Life: American Voices, Past and Present* (Layton, Utah: Gibbs M. Smith, A Peregrine

Smith Book, 1986), pp. 49, 51; Chadwick, *The Reformation*, pp. 193-94.

46. Carl F. Bowman, *Brethren Society: The Cultural Transformation of a "Peculiar People"* (Baltimore: Johns Hopkins University Press, 1995), pp. 17-18; Francis Bailey, *The Freeman's Journal, or The North-American Intelligencer*, 1 August 1781.

47. Bowman, *Brethren Society*, pp. 17-18.

48. Bowman, *Brethren Society*, p. 18.

49. Bowman, *Brethren Society*, p. 18.

50. Hostetler, *Hutterite Society*, pp. 119-27, 130.

51. Hostetler, *Hutterite Society*, pp. 126-27.

52. Hostetler, *Hutterite Society*, p. 127.

53. Hostetler, *Hutterite Society*, p. 128.

54. Hostetler, *Hutterite Society*, p. 129.

55. Hostetler, *Hutterite Society*, p. 129.

56. Hostetler, *Hutterite Society*, p. 129.

57. Hostetler, *Hutterite Society*, p. 129.

58. Hostetler, *Hutterite Society*, pp. 129-30.

59. "The Trial and Martyrdom of Michael Sattler," p. 100.

The
EGO IS ALWAYS
at the
WHEEL

ALSO BY DELMORE SCHWARTZ

From New Directions:
In Dreams Begin Responsibilities and Other Stories
Selected Poems: Summer Knowledge
Shenandoah (in *New Directions 32*)

From Other Publishers:
"I Am Cherry Alive," The Little Girl Sang
Last & Lost Poems. Edited by Robert Phillips
Letters of Delmore Schwartz. Edited by Robert Phillips
Portrait of Delmore: The Journals and Notes, 1939-1959.
Edited by Elizabeth Pollet
Selected Essays. Edited by Donald A. Dike
and David H. Zucker
Successful Love and Other Stories

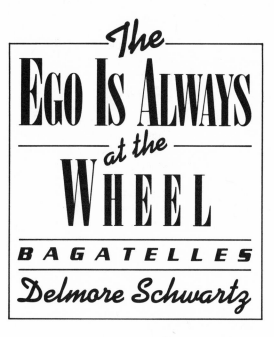

The
EGO IS ALWAYS
at the
WHEEL

BAGATELLES

Delmore Schwartz

EDITED BY ROBERT PHILLIPS

A New Directions Book

Manufactured in the United States of America
First published clothbound in 1986
Published simultaneously in Canada by
Penguin Books Canada Limited

Library of Congress Cataloging-in-Publication Data
Schwartz, Delmore, 1913-1966.
    The ego is always at the wheel.
    (A New Directions Book)
    Bibliography: p. 145
    I. Title.
PS3537.C79E4   1986   814'.52   85-28440
ISBN 0-8112-0983-0

New Directions Books are published for James Laughlin
by New Directions Publishing Corporation,
80 Eighth Avenue, New York 10011

SECOND PRINTING

ACKNOWLEDGMENTS

The following unpublished essays appear with the permission of the Beinecke Rare Book and Manuscript Library, Yale University, which houses the Delmore Schwartz Papers: "On the Telephone," "Dostoevsky and the Bell Telephone Company," "The Famous Elephant," "Publicity," "The Farmer Takes His Time," "An Author's Brother-in-Law," "The Naming of a Hotel," "Streetcar, the Metaphor," and "Memoirs of a Metropolitan Child, Memoirs of a Giant Fan."

The previously published essays appeared in the following magazines and books: "Existentialism: The Inside Story" (in different form and titled, "Does Existentialism Still Exist?"), *Partisan Review*, 15 (December 1948); "Paperbacks and the Elizabethan Parallel" (as "Speaking of Books"), *The New York Times Book Review*, January 17, 1954; "Survey of Our National Phenomena" in *The New York Times Magazine*, April 15, 1954; "Poetry Is Its Own Reward" (as "Two Problems in Writing of Poetry") in *Mid-Century American Poets*, ed. John Ciardi (Twayne Publishers, 1950).

The following essays were first published in *Vaudeville for a Princess and Other Poems* by Delmore Schwartz (New Directions, 1950): "The Ego Is Always at the Wheel," "The Difficulty of Divorce," "Hamlet, or There Is Something Wrong with Everyone," "Don Giovanni, or Promiscuity Resembles Grapes," "Iago, or the Lowdown on Life," and "Fun with the Famous, Stunned by the Stars."

My thanks are due to Griselda Ohannessian of New Directions Publishing Corporation for her encouragement and help with this collection.

Were it not presumptuous to dedicate another man's words to a third party, I would append a dedication page reading, "To Elizabeth Pollet—Delmore's wife and my friend—with gratitude."

R.P.

CONTENTS

FOREWORD

Delmore Schwartz appended Jonathan Swift's phrase, "*Vive la bagatelle*," to his most playful book of poetry and prose, *Vaudeville for a Princess*, and I think of the following essays as Schwartz's bagatelles—short pieces in a light style. They are distinctly different from those appearing in *Selected Essays of Delmore Schwartz* (1970; reprinted 1986). Those pieces were Schwartz's serious and public pronouncements on literature of the twentieth century—on general questions of poetry and criticism, as well as on individual fiction writers and poets. The present volume represents Schwartz in a less serious mood. The pieces seem to have been written primarily for his own amusement. He did publish a handful, as prose interludes between the poems of *Vaudeville for a Princess* (long out of print). He appended another to a selection of his poems in an anthology, and three others appeared in magazines. But the remainder were found among his uncatalogued papers now housed at Yale. Written in the 1940s and '50s, the most recent was dated 1958, fairly late in his writing career. He died in 1966.

Unlike his posthumous collection of poems, for which he made several tentative tables of contents, there is no evidence Schwartz planned to gather these prose pieces. Yet each had undergone numerous revisions, from handwritten drafts to corrected typescripts. On occasion I have had to choose from variant versions. I feel the pieces, as a little book, communicate much of the comic spirit and wisdom which endears Schwartz to readers. Like Thurber and Lardner, to whom he might in this instance be compared, Schwartz knew that the serious and the funny are one. For Schwartz, comedy was an escape—not from truth, but from despair. Time and again his comic sense constituted a leap into faith. In one of his last poems, written in 1961, "This Is a Poem I Wrote at Night,

Before the Dawn," he proclaims: "It is always darkness before delight!" Quite so. Schwartz used puns the way some poets employ enjambment—to extract a second meaning from a statement. In the pieces collected here one encounters a number of such epigrams, not the least memorable of which are, "A rolling stone gathers no remorse," and "Give me enough hope and I'll hang myself."

The personal essay seems a form especially congenial to Schwartz. It allowed his far-reaching imagination to play, even cavort. Witty, bright, full of satirical energy and verve, these amusing pieces at times may seem glib. But for the most part they are light-hearted and mocking views of the poet himself, of the literary world, and of the world-at-large.

Anything nourished his imagination. An ad for a mail-order bride prompts speculations on Kierkegaard and Freud. There are pieces on the American passion for automobile ownership, and a comic definition of existentialism. There is a piece ridiculing the laws which govern divorce (in which Schwartz pretends he is writing about the divorce of "a friend" rather than himself); and a confessional interpretation of Hamlet's character (concluding that the melancholy Dane was manic-depressive, a disorder for which "no one knows what the real causes . . . are, whether physical or mental or both. . . ."). Schwartz knew painfully well of what he was writing. Some may have forgotten it was he who first said, "Even paranoids have real enemies." His identification with Hamlet even becomes physical, writing of the Prince's "tendency to get fat in the face and thicken," a personal transformation for which the poet apologizes in his piece on getting his own photograph taken.

The reader will also find character sketches of Othello and Don Juan, as well as of the poet's twelve-year-old brother-in-law (here renamed Claude rather than Sylvester), and Marilyn Monroe. The poet had a bit of a fixation on the latter; he also wrote a poem, "Love and Marilyn Monroe," posthumously published in *Partisan Review* in 1976. Other subjects are the mixed blessings of the telephone, corporate executive seminars, the discomforts of being interviewed and photographed, the paperback revolution, and the vicissitudes of being a New York Giant fan. All are written in Schwartz's highly idiomatic style which lends an incongruous air to his serious subjects and personal theories—as when he concludes his Freudian discussion of Don Giovanni with these words: "All of these theories may or may not be true, but after one has reviewed all of them and weighed them critically, there is only one conclusion one can feel any certainty about, namely, that Giovanni was a Lesbian, that is to say, someone who likes to sleep with girls." Throughout, high seriousness lies just beneath the brittle surface. And Schwartz's prose is admirable for its freshness, as when he posits the unexpected adjective in the phrase, "indigestible cocktail parties," or when he recalls a streetcar from his youth, looking in its jangling voyage like both a schooner and a caterpillar.

These pieces reveal that Schwartz was passionate for personal glory as well as for poetry and the writing of poetry. The book is a bonus to admirers of Schwartz; few knew of the existence of these essays. In her admirable and knowledgeable review of *Letters of Delmore Schwartz*, Elizabeth Hardwick wrote in *The New York Times Book Review* that, inasmuch as that book followed the appearance of Schwartz's selected essays and a collection of his last poems, ". . . thus it seems we now have the whole of the writings."

Not so. There is still a considerable amount of writing to be evaluated for publication. Elizabeth Pollet's edition of

Schwartz's poetry journals is one extremely valuable project. Publication of his book-length, many-sided critical study of T.S. Eliot will probably occur in the near future. There are five verse plays which might be collected. Then there are unpublished novels, stories, and the interminable autobiographical poem, *Genesis, Book II*. Much of this material is not Schwartz at his best.

As Schwartz's literary executor, I am aware that the current and future flurry of publication (though good in itself) ultimately may not do his reputation much good. Letters, journals, essays, and plays do nothing to remove his neglect as a poet, and it *is* as a poet that Schwartz makes his greatest claim on posterity. Still, these books keep the coals of public interest glowing, so to speak, until they can be stoked by some future critic who will return to the poetry and newly assess it. There is no question Schwartz is undervalued, still, among the poets of his generation. He is represented by only two poems—both war-horses—in *The New Oxford Book of American Verse*, edited by Richard Ellman. And I was shocked to see he is not represented at all in the new *Harvard Book of American Poetry*, edited by Helen Vendler, while Lowell, Berryman, Jarrell, and newly-published poets like Amy Clampitt are. The omission of Schwartz merely suggests the absurdity of the attempt by any college, university press, or single critic—however eminent—to determine the literary tastes of a country as diverse as ours.

Until Schwartz the poet receives his due, we can sit back and savor his work in other forms. I make no claims for *The Ego Is Always at the Wheel* other than that it is entertaining and at times instructive. I think Schwartz would not mind at all seeing these pieces together and available at last.

—Robert Phillips

The
EGO IS ALWAYS
at the
WHEEL

Vive la bagatelle—*Swift*

THE EGO IS ALWAYS AT THE WHEEL

Cars are very important, even if one does not care very much about cars. This is because most people admire a handsome car very much. If one is an owner of a fine car, then one is regarded by the populace in general as being very successful and prosperous.

I myself never cared very much for cars, but as the years pass I can see how serious and significant a part they have played in my life. In 1929 when my family was rich, or supposed to be rich, I was given the gift of a Chrysler Royal coupe, brand-new. I did not know how to drive and our chauffeur had to teach me and the first thing I did at the wheel, turning the corner, was to drive into a truck, but slowly, so nothing bad happened. I have hardly had any accidents since then, for this beginning made me very cautious. I wanted to give up driving right then and there, but the wise chauffeur insisted that I continue, or otherwise I would never be able to drive a car.

I was full of pride in this beautiful car and went about in it, trying to find girls to ride with me and a friend. We were not very successful because we drove down Riverside Drive and the girls loitering there invariably preferred sailors when the fleet was in town. My friend said that this was because the navy spent money freely and without a care. Be this as it may, the car caused me no little sorrow because I expected girls to be very much attracted by it, but instead they were suspicious, cautious, and thought my friend and I eager only to make love. This was true enough, but what about the sailors?

After two years, during which time I suffered at the hands of the fair sex and also suffered because I expected girls to fall for my car, and suffered also because I was driving without a license and scared by every cop who glanced at me, I had to sell my car to pay my tuition fees at the university where I was supposed to be studying. I was cheated in the deal, but that's another story. The main point is that the depression had begun and that my family was not rich, as had been supposed, and I did not have the money to pay for the upkeep of the car.

It took me five years to get used to the idea that I was not what a relative termed a rich heir and the idea that the depression was not just an interval before a new period of prosperity. By that time I had accustomed myself to the idea of being without a car. All I wanted to do was to read books.

By 1938, I had read so many books that I wrote one. I felt so good that I went out and bought a car, a 1929 Ford. It was a good car, despite its age, and it gave me much pleasure and fostered no foolish, amorous expectations. At the end of the year I sold it for twenty-five dollars in credit. I was cheated again by an automobile dealer wise in the ways of the world. But still the car was a good thing.

In 1939, I lived during the winter at a summer resort and

had to buy a car again and I bought a 1928 Chevrolet. This was the best of all the cars so far as satisfaction went, although the motor was not all that it should have been. Driving from place to place in this car, I secured a very fine job, a much desired prize, and visited many illustrious and interesting persons. One of them was much struck by the fact that I drove a car at all. After I had visited him at his summer house in the mountains, he said to a friend of mine: *"He can drive a car!"* This shows the kind of impression I make on most human beings, partly because I look shy and helpless. I look that way very often because I am trying to figure out why the Giants did not win the pennant in 1928, or what would have happened if Germany had won the First World War, or what would have happened to me if not for the Great Depression which stopped me from being a rich young man. I also think of other things like that and find myself fascinated by all kinds of possibilities, if indeed they are possibilities. Strange that my abstracted and absent-minded look should make people think that I am shy and helpless: do they think I am not thinking *at all?* The fact is, I am passionate with reveries of glory and power, of riding up Fifth Avenue under great snowstorms of ticker-tape, in a beautiful open limousine, cheered by admiring throngs.

Anyway, I had to sell my third car, the 1928 Chevrolet, in 1940, because the police in the city in which I lived kept giving me tickets for parking outdoors all night, but I had to, for I did not have the money to pay for a garage. After the sale was concluded—and this time I was very cautious and cagey with the used car dealer—I felt that I was really slipping. After eleven years I had no car and I did not see how I was going to have a car very soon, but I had begun in 1929 with a very fine 1929 car.

Taxis are better, and less expensive, I figured during this period.

During the war a very rich friend often lent me his very expensive car, for at this time I was trying to impress a very cold and handsome young lady. She was not impressed since she did not like the way that I drove, and the truth is that my skill had decayed because of insufficient practice and because I had become very nervous as a result of all the ups and downs of life as I had known it.

Things went from worse to worst. I became so nervous that I was afraid to drive a car. But then at the darkest hour, I decided to buy a new car. This was quite recently, and the car belonged to a prosperous friend of mine who was afraid to sell it to me being aware of how nervous I was and thinking as others have that I was not the sort who could drive a car very well. He asked me politely if I still remembered how to drive, for he had seen me driving and had sat next to me in my 1928 Chevrolet in 1939. The sale was consummated after his natural hesitancy and the customary formalities. I secured an ownership license, license plates, and I would have taken a road test for a driver's license—my first one had expired four years before—except that one had to wait two weeks for an appointment and I had to go out of town immediately.

So there I was on the road again. *Allons!* I said to myself, as Walter Whitman used to say, once more without a driver's license just like in 1929 when I was too young to be permitted to get one in the State of New York which is very strict. And my emotions were pretty much the same—*le plus ça change, le plus c'est la même chose*—fear of the cops, bravado based on the probability and improbability of being halted, nervousness which doubtless went back to the strain of being hauled with great difficulty into this brave new world (it was a spectacular labor, I am told, and it was not until my mother accidentally kicked her father's photograph off the bedroom wall that the doctor said to my dubious and anxious father that everyone was going to be all right, a superficial remark if I ever heard one). Nevertheless, I drove with ever-increasing composure, and even, one might go so far as to say, a certain serenity, poise, and power, going north and feeling very good, despite the illegal character of my activity. For it had occurred to me to think of my first three cars, and when I compared them with this new car, I was very pleased. First the 1929 Royal coupe in 1929, next the 1929 Ford in 1930, third the 1928 Chevrolet in 1939-40, but now, after so many years of poverty and various kinds of oppression, chiefly internal, I owned a 1936 Buick in 1949.

There is no reason for wild optimism, but it would be hard to deny that I am slowly inching my way forward. It is true that this car is thirteen years old and at worst in the past my car was no more than twelve years old. But a Buick is a far, far better car than a Chevrolet, and next year if all goes well I think I may very well be able to trade it in for a 1941 Studebaker, with a radio and clock that really work. If this fair hope is fulfilled, I will only be nine years behind my starting point in 1929 and this will be progress indeed and who knows what the future may hold, so far as used cars go?

EXISTENTIALISM: THE INSIDE STORY

Is it not true that the discussion of the meaning of existentialism has been dying down? or at any rate is being taken more and more for granted, like cynicism, optimism, surrealism, alcoholism, and practically all other well-known topics of conversation?

If so, this is a dangerous state of affairs. For as soon as a philosophy is taken for granted, as soon as its meaning is assumed, then it begins to be misunderstood and misinterpreted. Philosophical idealism is a good example. It was once just as fashionable as existentialism and is now generally thought to have to do with those impractical people who believe in ideals and never amount to anything.

I propose a revival of interest in the meaning of existentialism because when everyone asks what something means, the possibilities of misunderstanding are, if not lessened, more controllable. Having studied existentialism in an offhand way since 1935, I become more and more convinced that its meaning can be reduced to the following formulation: *Existentialism means that no one else can take a bath for you.*

This example is suggested by Heidegger, who points out that no one else can die for you. You must die your own death. But the same is true of taking a bath. And I prefer the bath as an example to death because, as Heidegger further observes, no one likes to think very much about death, except indigent undertakers perhaps. Death is for most a distant event, however unpleasant and inevitable.

A bath, however, is a daily affair, at least in America. Thus it is something you have to think about somewhat everyday, and while you are thinking about it, and while, perforce, you are taking a bath, you might just as well be thinking about what existentialism means. Otherwise you will probably just be thinking about yourself, which is narcissism; or about other human beings, which is likely to be malicious, unless you are feeling very good; or worst of all, you may not be thinking at all, which is senseless and a waste of time.

Of course, there are other acts which each human being must perform for himself, such as eating, breathing, sleeping, making love, etc. But taking a bath seems to me the best of the lot because it involves the vital existentialist emphasis on choice: you can choose *not* to take a bath, you can waver in your choice, you can finally decide to take a bath, the whole drama of human freedom can become quite hectic or for that matter quite boring. But eating is hardy a matter of choice, except for the menu itself, nor is breathing which can be done not only without taking thought but while one is quite unconscious. As for making love, taking a bath is a better example because you can keep it clean, simple, free of fixations, perversions, inhibitions, and an overpowering sense of guilt.

Now despite the fact that most of the bathtubs which exist are in America, some Americans are not in the habit of taking baths for granted. I know of one American (formerly an existentialist, by the way) who avoids taking frequent baths because he feels that the taking of a bath is an *extreme situation*. (He is not averse to using existentialist arguments when it suits his torso, though in company he attacks existentialism.) He says that taking a bath is an extreme situation because God knows what may occur to you when you are in the tub; you may decide to drown yourself because existence, as existentialists say, is essentially *absurd*; you may decide to become a narcissist because of the pleasures of the warm and loving water. But there's no use listing all the catastrophes this fellow thinks may occur to anyone in the extreme situation of taking a bath.

So too with the bathtaking of a close friend of mine, who finds the taking of baths a matter of no little thought. He takes two baths a day, but he has to force himself to do so because there are so many other more important things to do (so it seems to him!) or which he feels he ought to do during the time occupied in taking a bath (note how the question of moral value enters at this point). It is a matter for much thought also because he has to decide whether to take a bath or a shower. He is afraid that sooner or later he will break his neck slipping on a cake of soap while taking a shower (which he prefers to a bath), although, on the other hand, he feels that in some ways it is better to take a shower than a bath because then he does not have to wash out the tub for others (*the others* are always important, as Sartre has observed), and in short the taking of baths is not a simple matter for him. Once I visited him while he was taking a shower, and while I was conversing with his wife in their handsome living-room, he kept crying out through the downpour of the shower: "Say, you know it's mighty lonesome in here." He wanted me to visit with him and keep him company (note the *aloneness* of the human situation as depicted by the existentialists), to converse with him. Consequently, after he had shouted his fourth appeal for my company, I had to go in and point out to him that we would have to shout at each other because of the noise of the shower and we shouted at each other often enough for more justifiable reasons.

In the upper class, as is well known, it is customary (I am told by friends who have soared to these circles at times ho, ho!) to take at least two baths a day, while in the lower middle class and working class this is less true, an observation I bring forward to show how important social and economic factors are; or, as the existentialists say, how all being is being-in-the-world, although they seem to think that the social and economic aspects of being-in-the-world are not so important as I am forced to think they are. Of course, some of the existentialists may have changed their minds during the second World War and the recent so-called peace.

The real difficulty in explaining what existentialism means flows from the basis of this philosophy, a basis which can be summarized in the following proposition: *Human beings exist.* They have an existence which is human and thus different from that of stones, trees, animals, cigar store Indians, and numerous human beings who are trying their best not to exist or not to be human.

If you are really human, if you really exist as a human being, you have no need of any explanation of existence or existentialism. In the meantime, the best thing to do is to keep on reading explanations of existentialism and existence.

As for me, I never take baths. Just showers. Takes less time.

ON THE TELEPHONE

The hubbub about television, of late, has been such, I think, as to conceal the fact that one of the most important things in life is the telephone. I've been unable to do much reading in recent years, but so far as I know, the telephone has not been the subject of any really serious consideration and analysis.

Yet people have been making telephone calls more than ever before (partly, we know, because there are more people than ever before), and all sorts of fantastic and fabulous things have been occurring as a result of the phone.

For example, the telephone company has become very cynical. The cynicism of the telephone company shows in the new edition of the telephone book in which, on page three, we are told how to cope with any situation in which our conversation on the phone is being recorded: "BEEP tone tells when telephone conversation is being recorded." The good book then continues by explaining that ". . . this signal (BEEP) is provided by the telephone company for your protection," and we are advised to hang up immediately, or ask our friend to disconnect his recorder.

This has serious implications. One is that our friends are not to be trusted. Another is that we don't know when to keep our mouths shut.

But to get back to the phone itself, its importance can be illustrated to some extent by explaining how it has been the bane of my existence. For a long time I lived in an academic community, and whenever anyone rang me about some casual matter, and said, "How are you?", instead of saying "Just fine" (which would have been untrue, but polite), I would tell them in lengthy detail just how I was, thus breaking the natural formality and rhythm of the conversation. Wasn't I ridiculous? I think this must have been why some people stopped calling me up. They were not *that* interested in how I was. And worse yet, if, in a careless moment, I said: "How are you?", some of these people, thinking that I wanted to be answered as I answered them, would then tell me in lengthy detail—but not as lengthy as mine. The result was that I was bored to death.

Then there is another practice, introduced, I believe, by Al Capone, the income tax expert, that of calling up someone and then hanging up, and doing this repeatedly. A friend of mine had a lady friend who used to do this in order to find out if he were being true to her. After he had left her in the evening and returned to his home, she would call him up as soon as he arrived at his domestic retreat. She suspected that he might go to visit some other lady. But she was ashamed of her suspicion. Hence, after hearing his preoccupied greeting, she hung up the receiver. This was her way of checking him in and the reason she did this awful thing was not because she had any real reason for distrusting him, but because she did not think that she herself was really loveable and deserving of fidelity. And she was right, as you can see.

Another thing about the phone is that it requires a certain fundamental naïveté. As is well-known, those who have studied philosophy and are really well-trained in the wisdom of the telephone think that there is some reason to doubt that anyone ever hears or understands what anyone else is saying. This is the so-called problem of knowledge. Of course, no one really believes this, otherwise they would not talk so much. But philosophers pretend that this is true because it is their profession (that is to say, the way they make their living) to make believe that everything has to be proven, nothing can be taken for granted. You have to be serious all the time. And this doctrine, that each being is separated from and cannot communicate with every other being, is celebrated in one part of a poem which is beginning to attract attention, *The Waste Land* by T.S. Eliot, one of the most promising poets of the present day. He writes:

> *I have heard the key*
> *Turn in the door once and turn once only*
> *We think of the key, each in his prison*
> *Thinking of the key, each confirms a prison*
> *Only at nightfall, aethereal rumours*
> *Revive for a moment a broken Coriolanus*

Now this shows one aspect of the fundamental naïveté necessary for using the telephone, since if one really believed the above lines, or the philosophers, one might never make a phone call. Or if one did, one would be logically inconsistent. Nonetheless I notice that most philosophers use the phone just as much as anyone else.

Another aspect of the naïveté I have in mind is shown by what happened to a friend of mine years ago when the dial telephone was introduced. His mind was so complicated that he could not figure out how the dial could work. He thought that when he dialed ABC or XYZ, all three letters would be rung and thus the call could not possibly go through. It was only after six months of avoiding dial phones that he explained his plight to a simple-minded acquaintance for whom he had little respect (and in whom he was thus not ashamed to confide), and the simple-minded fellow explained to him how his mind was too complicated. As a result, this complicated and sophisticated friend of mine had a dial phone installed in his home immediately and made calls like mad for the next ten days.

And yet it should not be supposed that the telephone is entirely an unfortunate and misleading instrument. The most touching thing about it, I think, is the way in which it shows how eager human beings are to talk to each other, no matter what they have to say and even if they don't always and invariably say favorable things. People are really very friendly and they love to hold telephone conversations if they have nothing better to do. And as a friend of mine recently remarked to me, the telephone is wonderful when you are lonesome. Without leaving the house you can call up any friend and talk things over.

There was a period when I had no phone, the result, I believe, of economic determinism, or to put it plainly, I just could not afford one. Consequently, it was supposed by acquaintances who occupied higher income tax brackets (I occupied none whatever) that I was unfriendly. This was certainly untrue. The truth was that *I* thought *they* were unfriendly, otherwise they would understand my economic plight and find some other way to reach me. Sometimes when someone really wanted to get me, they would send me Western Union telegrams which invariably scared the life out of me, because I thought someone had died and I was being told to rush to the funeral. Usually these wires were invitations to indigestible cocktail parties or requests for book reviews in which I was expected to emulate Sainte-Beuve in forty-eight hours while dealing with some poor author's latest catastrophic drive toward fame and fortune.

In short, the telephone is far from an unmixed blessing, although it certainly *is* a blessing. I don't think that Alexander Graham Bell really knew what he was getting us into. Just think how the telephone has transformed the whole so-called art of playwriting. As a friend of mine once said to me: "What a pity that Henrik Ibsen did not know about the telephone." He was making a very wise remark. If you want to find out just how much wisdom there is in that observation, get away from your phone, get a room in a hotel, tell them not to put through any calls, and start rereading Ibsen's plays, if you can stand them.

DOSTOEVSKY AND THE BELL TELEPHONE COMPANY

It is six years since the autumn afternoon when I received an entirely unexpected letter from the University of Pennsylvania. I was very pleased to get the letter, and I was also quite astonished and somewhat perplexed. For the letter was an invitation to lecture on *The Brothers Karamazov:* The lecture was part of a special program for a group of junior executives of the Bell Telephone Company. The junior executives had come to study for a full year at the university, and my own lecture was to be part of a course on the masterpieces of world literature. The sum paid for the lecture was extremely generous and indeed all arrangements made by the Bell Company were bountiful to the point of luxury. The chosen executives were being paid for a full year's salary, and all their expenses were an additional part of the company's largesse. They were also provided with suites in the best hotels and they had the privilege of making free long distance calls.

Before describing the lecture I gave, perhaps I had better

explain—if it is, indeed, an explanation and not a further problem, perplexity, and complication—what I learned only after I had given the lecture: The higher powers of the Bell Company had decided during the previous year that these junior executives suffered from "patterns of over-conformity." This is a direct quotation and it explained nothing whatever to me, for a variety of reasons: I will mention just one. Like many other human beings, I had long suffered from the impression that the very conception of over-conformity was virtually inconceivable to the heads of great businesses; it was, I had long supposed, as foreign to the mind of a tycoon as a passionate interest in the fiction of Dostoevsky or—to be more extreme and more exact—Robert Bridges' views of Milton's methods of scanning blank verse.

Perhaps this is—or was—unjust and shows how shallow, ignorant, unjust, and unimaginative I am to the sovereigns of the business community, to say almost nothing of the other ways in which I am an intellectual snob. At any rate, rightly or wrongly, I was sufficiently caught in the toils of my own limited powers of observation and imagination to suppose that distress about patterns of over-conformity was not the complete explanation, nor the sole reason for the presence of a group of junior executives at the University of Pennsylvania. After I had given my lecture, I entertained a view which is, I should insist, hardly more than an hypothesis, or perhaps that is the wrong word and gives too much dignity to what is merely a guess.

The guess or hypothesis was that the management—to use the term in which the management itself delights—of the Bell Telephone Company was distressed by a serious loss of social prestige, rather than, or more than, by patterns of over-conformity. If, for example the president or vice president of the Bell Telephone Company in a major American city went to a dinner party and heard the name of Dostoevsky bruited about, he might very well be likely to suppose that the conversation concerned a Soviet delegate to the U.N. And if he were so imprudent as to enter the conversation, thinking of Dostoevsky in this light, the possibilities of confusion, embarrassment, and embarrassed silence—or an effort to change the subject—were colossal. If the executive's ignorance showed itself in this or some other way, then he suffered a loss of social and cultural prestige which must be intolerable to the Bell management. For to be the president of a Bell company had been, for generations, a mark of genuine eminence, superior status, and unquestionable knowledge. Obviously such eminence was much reduced, and perhaps annihilated, when it became clear to others that the man on top was an ignoramus in matters of high culture, a human being who was not only ignorant, but misinformed and confused in matters of high culture and men of the greatest creative genius. The possibility of error and delusion was fearful and boundless. It was all too easy to suppose that Leopardi was the name of an excellent Italian typewriter, that Renoir was the name of an expensive French sports car, that Olivetti was a great lyrical poet, that William Saroyan wrote *The Divine Comedy*—to say almost nothing again about identifying Hegel and the bagel, the zeitgeist and zwieback, Charlotte Brontë and charlotte russe, chop suey and Tschaikovsky and Kung-Fu-Tse, Charles Lamb and lamb chop.

It should be clear that I made myself extremely nervous merely by thinking of how many misapprehensions were all too probable.

It must be said once again that this is no more than a guess based upon brief and unconnected conversational remarks. But it is true that the Bell Company's special program of studies has been reported in print by others, and although the accounts I have read are full of an optimism, I myself do not feel hopeful about the present and the immediate future of high culture. Nevertheless nothing in these accounts suggests that my guess is incorrect.

As Marianne Moore says in one of her poems, commenting on the school-boy holler, "Caesar crossed the Alps *cum diligentia:* Caesar crossed the Alps on a diligence." Miss Moore comments: "It is not that one is daft about the right meaning, but that this familiarity with the wrong meaning puzzles one."

I was wrong enough, however, when I devoted a whole month rereading Dostoevsky, typing out the lecture after consulting every literary cricket in reach who had ever written about Dostoevsky and *The Brothers Karamazov.* Among these writers were not only Marilyn Monroe and Arthur Miller, both stars of screen and fiction, but also Arnold Bennett and André Gide. Both great novelists had said that *The Brothers Karamazov* was the greatest of all novels; this remarkable agreement among very different minds seemed to me an excellent dramatic beginning for a lecture.

By the time the lecture was half delivered, I became aware that what I was saying was not likely to make very much of an impression upon Bell Company junior executives, if I knew anything about them. When the lecture was over and when what was supposed to be the question period proved to be, for the most part, a prolonged, almost unbroken, and painfully embarrassed silence which distressed everyone—although probably not in the same way—I became aware that I might very well have given the lecture without opening the novel. And then when the silence of the question period had continued until it seemed as positive and loud as thunder, one executive—moved, I think, by courtesy rather than curiosity—drawing upon all his reserves of ingenuity and tact, signified his desire, so to speak, to ask a quesion. "Say Doc," (Doc was me) "is Russian life really like that?" he inquired with no eagerness whatsoever. I drew forth a copy of the *New York Journal American* which I had unwittingly brought with me, and after scanning the headlines, reading them aloud, and becoming aware that I was getting nowhere, answered with what was a peculiar smugness in the context, because the subject was a novel full of fear, hatred, violence, horror, culminating in murder—the smugness was merely a feeling of profound relief and reprieve—that life was like that everywhere. The question itself was enough to make me reasonably certain that the prolonged silence of the question period was not caused solely by a poor or poorly-given lecture.

It was my impression, I answered, that the quality and character of life in America as well as in Russia—and in all truth everywhere, so far as I knew—was precisely what Dostoevsky had represented it to be in his greatest novel. There was one other question—about whether reading *T.B.K.* had not been pretty tough going, Doc—which made me aware, as perhaps I should have been all along, that my captive audience had been so bored and trapped by Dostoevsky that they had been unable to read it from beginning to end. Feodor was an unbearable bore.

Another student spoke out as we began to get up; what he said was a comment rather than a question, and had to do with I.A. Richards, who had been the first guest lecturer, or one of the first, and had devoted himself to a detailed elucidation of one of T.S. Eliot's poems entitled "A Cooking Egg." His elucidation seemed to have distressed the Bell junior ex-

— 21 —

ecutive, not only because it made Eliot's poem extremely complicated but because Richards thought extreme complications entirely justified a poem when it was a good poem. The comment—which for a time perplexed me—was that the Bell commentator was delighted to hear that I felt as I did (although I did not) about Professor Richards, and he was sure most of the rest of the bunch was also quite pleased.

I began to say that I admired the work of I.A. Richards very much and then stopped, feeling that this would merely contribute to the confusion. I had, in my lecture, spoken briefly and in passing, of a sentence in a book by Richards published in 1925. Richards had remarked that the problems which concerned the characters in Dostoevsky's fiction would probably be outmoded by science and psychoanalysis.

My own remark in the course of my lecture was merely that I felt that Professor Richards no longer believed this to be true. What I said in qualified admiration was misunderstood as irony and seized upon as a genuine bond between the junior executive and myself.

A truly genuine bond appeared soon after when I was invited to the luxurious hotel suite provided for those who had participated in the program. I was asked—shyly, with extreme tact, as if the one who asked the question were walking not upon ordinary eggs but swans' eggs—if I liked to drink???? Under ordinary circumstances, this question would have carried me so far from reality that several days' forced marches would have been necessary to make possible my return to actuality. But my desire for a drink, after the trials of the lecture and its aftermath, was too intense and too impatient to permit the question to be regarded in perspective: I answered quickly and concisely, concerned only about getting a drink as soon as possible: "Oh, I drink like a fish."

There seems to be some misunderstanding about those who read books having no time for guzzling; no class of people are more abundantly provided with time for drinking than readers of books.

Before long, choice spirits had brought about a state of union, sympathy, and communication far greater and far more cordial and far more profound than Dostoevsky's masterpiece. And as I began to feel not only no pain but extremely pleased—and, as I think the Bell boys had decided that I was virtually one of the Bell boys too and not the haughty and supercilious egghead they expected anyone who lectured on Dostoevsky to be—I began to ask questions about "just *what* an important executive of the Bell company did—just what did he do which made him an important executive?" Although I conceded my ignorance—what else could I do?—I pointed out that it was difficult to see what a Bell executive did, after certain points had been reached. There could not be very much to do, I said stupidly, except to install more and more telephones, and surely this hardly required highly trained executive skill, knowledge, or, to use the American word, know-how.

A good deal of hesitation—and exchange of looks—preceeded the answer to my question, almost as if an explicit answer would involve undesirable disclosures, such as might occur when matters of military security and secrecy were at stake. Finally, I was answered with extreme reticence, with one word, "Electronics." I understood that the hesitation was a kind of shyness, an attitude on the part of all junior executives which they strive in vain to conceal. The answer was somewhat unsatisfactory because of my natural ignorance of the nature of electronics. To say that electronics was a recondite and obscure subject to me was tantamount to describing the Black Hole of Calcutta as a Crystal Palace. I toyed, for a moment, with the senseless thought of suggesting that anyone capable of mastering electronics might very well be sympathetic enough to master the complications of T.S. Eliot's poem and the complexity of I.A. Richards elucidation.

The next year, I was once again invited to lecture on *The Brothers Karamazov* to a new group of junior executives of the Bell Telephone Company. I revised the lecture I had written the year before—in the light, or the darkness perhaps—of what had occurred the year before. And I was wrong again. For the new group of junior executives were a very different lot. They were serious, curious, determined, and what was perhaps most important of all, their wives had come with them and were reading the same books as their husbands. As I spoke I became aware, with growing amazement, that my listeners were listening in a state of devout concentration. And when the question period began, Dostoevsky's novel and my lecture were the subjects of one difficult question after another. Thus, since I had said that one of Dostoevsky's themes was the reality of good and evil, and since I had said that if one human being murdered another human being (however worthless or evil the victim), the murderer found himself in a state of being which was extremely unpleasant and far inferior to the state he had known prior to becoming a murderer, and this was true whether or not his crime was discovered and he was punished by others. The crime of murder was the cause of inescapable guilt even when the human being was like Ivan Karamazov, who had merely desired the murder to occur, or had, like Dmitri Karamazov, actually committed the murder. Everyone involved, perhaps even the victim, experienced a sense of unbearable guilt.

This observation did not seem to be quite true to a Bell

junior executive: "Do you mean to say, Doc"—I was still Doc despite the change of attitudes—he inquired, "that all of us have a sort of built-in moral sense?" He illustrated his doubt by referring to the tycoons who had made great fortunes during the second half of the nineteenth century. They had often been, he asserted, wholly ruthless and unscrupulous in getting what they wanted: yet there was no sign that they had been troubled, at any time, by unbearable guilt. The questioner's example had been John D. Rockefeller, Sr. I answered by speaking of an incident in Rockefeller's life which I had come upon a month before in the third volume of Santayana's memoirs.

I explained that the great philosopher, George Santayana, was a good friend of C. H. Strong, another professor of philosophy and the husband of Rockefeller's daughter; and that one time Mr. Rockefeller, his son-in-law, and his daughter invited Santayana to dinner. The dinner occurred in Paris, and Santayana had just returned from his native Spain. Having been informed of this, the great Standard Oil magnate began to converse with Santayana by asking him what the population of Spain was. And when Santayana told him, Rockefeller's comment was—it seemed to me unbelievable, but it was true—that there were not enough Standard Oil Company units in Spain.

I was unable to tell just how effective this answer was. It was sufficiently effective, however, to inspire another question, a question which is, I think, relevant not only to the purpose of the Bell Telephone Company program, but to American life as a whole.

"Everything you say may be true, Doc," the questioner admitted. "Dostoevsky may be one of the greatest of writers, and *The Brothers Karamazov* is probably the masterpiece you say it is: But who am I going to talk to about Dostoevsky and *The Brothers Karamazov?*"

My answer was spontaneous and sanguine. I do not know whether or not it was adequate or justified and hence I only want to present the answer itself, making no comment upon it and jumping to no conclusions.

"Perhaps," I said, "in twenty years' time you will be able to discuss Dostoevsky's book with rising generations of junior executives of the Bell Telephone Company."

CAUGHT BY THE CAMERA'S EYE

The two related problems of photographs and interviews were merged once sometime ago, when a new book of mine came out, and a national magazine called up and said they wanted to take a new picture of me and also have an interview which they could run with the review of my book, which as I had already been told, was very favorable. But I was engaged that day, in a way which, though it makes me sheepish, must be confessed. I was going to a double-header between the Giants and the Dodgers and I had been looking forward to it all morning and I did not feel like not going. I suggested to the secretary, who was trying to arrange an appointment for photograph and interview, that I had an unavoidable doctor's appointment. She seemed both astonished and hurt because, as I later discovered, it was most peculiar, unfriendly, uncooperative (perhaps even unAmerican?) for anyone to try to dodge any kind of publicity in this national magazine, and she herself felt that I was expressing a certain attitude of disdain toward the great importance of this magazine with which she identified herself and which had a circulation of more than three million readers, though most of them could not possibly care very much about what was in my book. She tried to explain to me that no other appointment was possible because the magazine had to go to press before tomorrow, but I was in a hurry to get to the Polo Grounds, and I am afraid that I must have seemed rude to her.

This magazine then secured one of those old *Vogue* magazine photographs from the publisher of the book, and the next week there I was, false as ever, and handsome as I have never been (thank God, because women don't really like good-looking men). I had to point out to some ironic friends that not only was the photograph taken twelve years before, but also that I had not looked that way even then, it was all the result of the *Vogue* lighting and the *Vogue* photographer. I had to say this because some of my friends, who did not know me back then, seemed to feel sorry for me and seemed to think I had declined very much or aged, becoming stout-faced and heavy-set. So I was remorseful about not having a new photograph taken which would destroy the delusions created and sustained by the old ones, and I felt again that I must not permit my passion for major league baseball to interfere so much with other far more important matters.

As a result of this sad experience, I resolved to have my picture taken again at the next inexpensive opportunity, which soon occurred. There was a party for some visiting foreign poets—the Sitwells—and another national magazine decided to take pictures of all the poets who could be induced to come to this party. I went to the party, and there were a great many more important poets than I present; it looked as if my picture would not be taken, which did not trouble me because I was involved in sampling as much of the free and excellent hootch as I could. But then, at the last moment it turned out that another poet was necessary for the big group photograph, and I was summoned and torn away from my favorable position near the supply of firewater, and seated next to a poet [Randall Jarrell] to whom I had written just about a month before. I had had to explain to this excellent poet what I thought was wrong about his new play in verse, and my letter was brief and of necessity unconvincing, I guess, for he began to argue with me. To answer him I had to turn my head away from the camera, thus driving the photographer to distraction, for she kept crying out, begging me not to turn my head. But what could I do when my fellow poet was telling me that my sense of rhythm was probably in decline because I'd told him that he had used a form of versification which would hardly sustain itself across the brilliant footlights.

Moved by the pleas of the photographer, I remarked to the poet that I had often been wrong in the criticism of poetry, and perhaps I was wrong again. A certain irony, delightful to me, rose in my voice, and my fellow-poet looked very blank, or very stern, and it was then, smiling at my own evasion and reply, that I turned my head, and was photographed, looking rather gleeful, I must say. Anyone who sees that picture may think that I am a very cheery person and wonder about the great sorrow which is one of the leading themes of my work. This is the explanation: My fellow-poet's stubbornness in the face of criticism, my agility in turning the tables on him, and also the whiskey I had gulped hurriedly just before because I've always felt the truth of the truism that everything good in life is free.

POETRY IS ITS OWN REWARD

Questions about the practice of writing poetry make me very nervous because my answers look very strange after a newspaper reporter has rendered them. For instance, one time I replied to a question about meter by saying that there was no such thing as free verse, but only different kinds of rhythm. By the time this careless remark reached the printed page, it turned out that I had denied the existence of poems which were called free verse. This inexactitude may not seem important, but I feel that there is too much misunderstanding in the world as it is, and if that is the best that can be done by way of accurate repetition, I would rather shut up. However, it is necessary that one be polite, no matter what or how great the provocation. This requirement of politeness nearly ruined me once, however, when I was questioned as to whether the most important element in modern poetry was the intellectual factor or the emotional factor. Naturally I was stupefied. But politeness made me reply that it was just like the weather, sometimes it was too hot, sometimes it was too cold, sometimes it was just plain boring, and the less attention one paid to it, the better. My questioner, a very kind lady, who was just trying to make conversation, looked so alarmed at my answer that I hastened to assure her that Plato and Dryden were wrong when they declared that poets were practically insane. The next questioner was the feature writer, whatever that is, for a fashion magazine which printed literary prattle and the like to break the flow of gorgeous garment prose. Needless to say, I was on guard. The first question was about how I had decided to become a poet, so I explained that as an infant in the cradle I had cried loudly and received immediate and unanimous attention; consequently, putting two and two together, I had tried crying out loudly in public and in blank verse, and the results had on the whole been most gratifying. My questioner seemed to like this answer very much, for she wrote it down quickly in shorthand and then inquired as to the greatest influence upon me. I was about to say Shakespeare and the Depression of 1929-1937, but this was all too true, and since the truth had been distorted so often in all previous exchanges, I answered pre-natal experiences, for this was the first thing that came into my head. She took it as a *double entendre*, I think, for she left in a rage.

Since then, feeling badly about how all these well-meant inquisitions have turned out, I've given the whole subject cool and careful thought. The chief dangers, I've decided, are as follows: One may be too technical; or fleeing from technical observations and shop-talk, one may become oracular and thus very pretentious about poets as unacknowledged legislators and similar braggadocio, and from this extreme, one swings to facetiousness and receives a sickly, uneasy grin because poets are supposed to be very serious; and then, worst of all, one becomes too personal, thus infuriating other poets, although other readers just love these intimate disclosures.

Conscious of these dangers, and others I have not troubled to mention, I've often resorted to or been reduced to silence. But I feel now that no amount of circumspection will protect me, so I might as well speak freely. I chose two professional problems which have long occupied me.

One of these problems concerns itself with how much poetry one ought to write and how much one ought to publish. After much reflection, I've decided that one ought to write as much as possible and publish as little as possible. The latter conclusion follows from the glum fact that most poetry is likely to be bad, if judged by any standards which would justify the assertion that some poetry is good. On the other hand, one ought to write as much as possible banking on the law of averages because, among other reasons, there is no way of telling in advance whether the poem one writes is going to be good. Moreover, the writing of bad poems is for many poets a way of arriving at the writing of good poems. By publishing only work which one is reasonably comfortable about, or work which is in an idiom one no longer cultivates, one avoids the remorse of looking at one's bad poems in print and the paralyzing effects which may ensue. Horace advises one to wait for nine years before publishing a poem, and a very gifted modern poet told me that it is best to publish as much as possible, for one can always write more poems. Both pieces of advice may be good for some poets or good under certain conditions, but for most poets to wait, to be patient, to re-write and to keep looking at one's poems is the best possible method of procedure, if one is interested in writing good poems rather than in being regarded as a poet. There is nothing wrong in wanting to be known as a poet, but the desire to write good poems is more fruitful in the long run. Many good poets have been spoiled by the belief that they had to rush into print with a new book every year, and only a few have been weakened by revision, patience, and privacy.

This question is important in itself now, since the example of Auden has intensified the natural desire to appear in print very often; and it is a significant problem also because in trying to face it, one has to face the whole problem of the nature of poetry.

So too with the second problem, the relationship of any modern poet to his audience and to the well-known difficulty of modern poetry, a difficulty which obviously involves the audience. Anyone who wants to understand modern poetry can do so by working about half as hard as he must to learn a language or to acquire any new skill or to learn to play bridge well. The real problem is the effect upon the poet himself of the reader's feeling that modern poetry is difficult. His frequent response of late has been one of panic, a panic which leads to false moves and desperate oversimplifications. One fashionable tendency has been to try to write poetry which would be intelligible to any audience. And meanwhile the extent of the difficulty has somehow increased in the public's mind, perhaps because the public has been preoccupied with matters other than literature. For a long time, *The Waste Land* seemed the perfect example of modern poetry's obscurity, but nowadays even the beautifully lucid poems of Robert Frost are said to be obscure. Perhaps this development is all to the good, since it may prevent poets from forcing themselves to try to be popular. But the fundamental problem presents itself falsely as long as it is supposed that the kind of poetry one produces is solely a matter of choice or will. Choice and will are involved, of course, but there is also present a large and inescapable relationship, a relationship which may well be prior because it has had a great deal to do with making the poet interested in writing poetry from the very start. Any modern poet exists in an inescapable relationship to all modern *and* modernist poetry which has been written since Baudelaire. He can choose to disregard or forget about this complicated relationship, but if he does, he is depriving himself of what is an important part of his inheritance as a poet, and also a powerful presence in the minds of everyone who is capable of reading poetry.

Consequently the modern poet is bound to be drawn in two apparently opposed directions. On the one hand, it is natural that he should want to write as directly and clearly as Yeats and Frost at their best (which is not to forget that their directness and clarity was accomplished only by means of a great deal of intellectual toil and obscure delvings). On the other hand, he is bound to be drawn toward an emulation of the marvelous refinements in the uses and powers of language which have occurred since the Symbolists first appeared.

The best convenient example of this cultivation of language is this little poem which appears in James Joyce's *Ulysses:*

> *White thy fambles, red thy gan,*
> *And thy quarrons dainty is.*
> *Couch a hogshead with me then.*
> *In the darkmans clip and kiss.*

(I choose this example not only for its convenient brevity, but also because it is an omen or beginning of *Finnegans Wake,* an overwhelming work which, if it concludes an epoch, also initiates a new one.) The obscurity of the little poem in

Ulysses is not reduced very much by its context in the novel. And even when the reader finds out (as he may not unless he reads Stuart Gilbert's commentary on *Ulysses*), that the words he does not understand, or only imperfectly understands, are gypsy slang, he may be disturbed by the poem or resent the author's use of unfamiliar and special words. Indeed, it can be argued (in a misleading way or in an illuminating one) that the beauty of this poem and the powerful emotion it communicates come through best of all when the reader does not know exactly what the exact gypsy meanings of the words are. For example, "couch a hogshead" means "lie down and sleep," and if one knows this in advance, some of the richness of connotation may be blocked off.

Every modern poet would like to be direct, lucid, and immediately intelligible, at least most of the time. In fact, one of the most fantastic misconceptions of modern literature and modern art in general is the widespread delusion that the modern artist does not want and would not like a vast popular audience, if this were possible without the sacrifice of some necessary quality in his work. But it is often not possible. And every modern poet would also like to be successful, popular, famous, rich, cheered on Broadway, sought by Hollywood, recited on the radio, and admired by Mr. J. Donald Adams. The lack of popularity does not arise from any poet's desire to punish himself and deprive himself of these glorious prizes and delectable rewards. The basic cause is a consciousness of the powers and possibilities of language, a consciousness which cannot be discarded with any more ease than one can regain one's innocence.

Some will doubtless continue to be irritated by the cultivation of language of which Joyce's poem is a somewhat extreme instance. And they will waste time, mind, and energy in defensive attitudes, denouncing or denying the virtues of this kind of writing.

And some will try to imitate and extend literally and mechanically the direction which Joyce represents.

And some will try to find a point at which the clarity of Yeats can be sought at the same time as one seeks the richness which Joyce possessed.

This last effort or ambition may be as quixotic and contradictory as an attempt to square the circle. But given the consciousness of literature likely in anyone who wants to write good poetry, anything less than the reconciliation of these extremes is far from enough. As some Indian chief once said on a visit to the White House after he had had two portions of everything but remained hungry: "A little too much of everything is just enough for me."

Orpheus once visited a colleague. His name was Agathon and he was a famous poet and critic of the time. Indeed he was much better known than Orpheus then, for the latter had not yet attracted to himself the widespread publicity which followed upon his sensational adventures in trying to get his wife to return to him.

Orpheus showed Agathon his most recent work, hoping for praise and admiration, but requesting a critical opinion.

"Frankly," said Agathon, "these poems are worthless. Even a fellow-poet like myself has a hard time understanding them. You can imagine what the common reader will and will not make of them. Why don't you write the way the old boys did? *This is not what the public wants.*"

"I do my best," said Orpheus meekly (he was very disappointed but grateful for his friend's candor), "I write whatever I can."

This story is endless. I hope to discuss it at greater length in the future. One must not be deceived by Orpheus' subsequent career which was largely in the nature of an escapade and *tour de force*. Every genuine poet is now in the same boat as Orpheus was then. Agathon was also right to say what he did say. What would have been the point of being other than sincere, if that was the way he felt?

"*Amor omnia vincit,*" muttered Orpheus under his breath as he left, "love always wins out. Poetry is its own reward. Maybe Agathon is right. Maybe he is wrong."

Obviously the preceding interview may be interpreted in several different ways.

THE FARMER TAKES HIS TIME

Reading the newspaper every day is the habit of so many human beings that it cannot be the luxury—the dangerous luxury, perhaps—that it is beginning to become for me. Other readers must be able to regard the news with less seriousness or more indifference than I do. The most recent item which made me wonder whether I ought not to stop reading the news every day was not a matter of great international significance: It had nothing to do with the Cold War, the Congo, the Soviet Union, or Cuba's foreign policy, for I have long expected to be bewildered, at the very least, and very often shocked, by international and national events. And when I read of Castro's attacks on the United States during recent months, I felt entirely prepared or rather braced, since the newspapers had reported more than two years ago that it was commonly believed in Havana that "Fidel is in a state of exaltation."

The news story which troubled me was of another kind: It appeared in *The New York Times*, which gave it the status of sobriety, respectability, and freedom from sensationalism which one hardly expects, or should expect when reading, let us say, the *New York Daily News*. And it concerned a personal matter, the search of a farmer for a wife. Before I quote the news story verbatim so that others can judge whether my distress was justified, I should explain, I think, that the topic of marriage and the related topic of divorce has long fascinated me for a variety of personal reasons which are of no interest to anyone but myself. In the past, however, the news of marriage or of divorce was the cause of curiosity, wonder, amazement, pleasure, dismay, and at times, amusement, but I did not feel profoundly disturbed. When I read, at least ten years ago, how a wife's divorce was based upon the accusation that, when she nursed her child, her husband made a special point of commenting on her fulfillment of a necessary maternal duty by mooing, I merely felt curiosity about what the real cause of the couple's estrangement was. This was true of a like instance, a divorce suit in which the wife asked for a divorce because her husband, a well-known author, told her each morning at breakfast that he was a far greater writer than William Shakespeare: I wondered, among other things, how the husband had described his literary gifts during the courtship which presumably preceded the marriage. Had he feigned a modesty which he did not possess for the sake of winning the lady? So too I was much impressed to read, some five years ago, in an interview with the press, that Miss Shelley Winters had said: "It was so cold last winter that I almost got married." This remark seemed to me to be the precise statement of a genuine insight.

The item in *The New York Times* became more distressing each time I read it. After the fourth reading, it made me wonder how much I knew of the nature of reality, human beings, human beings who are farmers in Wisconsin, and the character of American life. But let other readers judge whether I was disturbed to an unwarranted degree. Perhaps I should not have been disturbed at all:

FARMER WANTS WIFE
8,000 APPLY IN VAIN

Grantsburg, Wis. (A.P.)—Arthur Birnstengel, a hard-working 58-year-old farmer has no bad habits—but he does have one problem:

He can't pick out a wife.

But not for lack of applicants.

Since 1945 he has received more than 8,000 letters from women interested in marrying him. The mail started coming when Mr. Birnstengel wrote a letter to his Congressman asking for help. He had been married twice but was left alone with a 5-year-old boy, Artie, in 1945. He needed a wife to help rear the boy.

His Congressman, Alvin E. O'Konski, gave the letter to the news services and Mr. Birnstengel's plight was described around the world.

Letters came airmail, special delivery, and postage due. He read every letter and answered about 1,000. Some correspondence lasted three or four letters.

"Many of the first letters looked good but things usually changed on the second or third letter," he says.

Mail slowed to a few letters a week during the past summer. The letters are stored in large cardboard boxes. Each envelope has been neatly opened with scissors and is classified by its faults—"Churchy," "Smoker," "Drinker," "Too Young," "Too Old"—are some of them.

The "Just Right" category is empty. But it will take only one such letter to end the problem that has stymied him for fifteen years.

The Ego Is Always at the Wheel

I had better say immediately that it seemed likely—more than that, it seemed quite probable—that the intention of the newspaperman who wrote this piece was comic, although he was also inspired by motives of sympathy and a desire to help Mr. Birnstengel. And it may be that the passing of the years has weakened my sense of humor and heightened a long-existing tendency to be too serious about virtually everything. Nevertheless, this human interest story seems to me not only not funny, but profoundly depressing. The most intelligible and useful sentence in the entire piece is intelligible and useful *only* if an error in spelling has occurred and the next-to-last sentence in the entire piece is intelligible and useful *only* if an error in spelling has occurred and the next-to-last sentence really should read, "The 'Just Write' category is empty." But even if this sanguine emendation is correct, Mr. Birnstengel's plight and problem remain quite serious. It should be clear after fifteen years that, in all likelihood, Mr. Birnstengel's problem is not solely the need of a wife. For one thing, his son Artie is now twenty years of age. What Mr. Birnstengel needs at present is not a wife, but a constant flow of letters from unmarried women who are sufficiently eager to embrace "the ancient and honorable estate" of matrimony to be willing to enter into a correspondence with an unknown stranger who is a farmer in Grantsburg, Wisconsin. Indeed, it seems likely enough that Mr. Birnstengel's problem and plight have not only remained serious, but have become desperate. For the news story notes that Mr. Birnstengel has been getting only a few letters a week during the past summer, and sooner or later, it seems reasonable to predict, his mail will diminish to nothing at all unless something occurs to alter the present situation and demonstrate that Mr. Birnstengel's intentions are matrimonial and not epistolary, or worse.

Perhaps I am wrong, and Mr. Birnstengel is literally a careful and prudent man who wants to be sure that he is marrying the right woman. On the other hand, it is surely not wholly unfair to suppose that he might be regarded by some as a man who hesitates and has been lost in indecision for fifteen years. Again, he might be viewed as one who, to judge by his "categories," has standards which are so high that they can be compared to the extremely elevated standards of the heroines and heroes in the novels of Henry James who often hesitate to get married, more often than not, for five hundred, six hundred and seven hundred pages—and then sometimes don't get married at all, although marriage preoccupies them far more than any other part of life. A famous critic once made a comment about these Jamesian heroes and heroines which may seem extreme, since it is solely a question of fictional conduct: He said that if most human beings went through the same process of hesitation, critical analysis, and delay, the human species would soon cease to exist. It is a fact, however, that Mr. Birnstengel's son Artie has been reared without the help of a stepmother. It might be argued that the news story says nothing to suggest that Artie has not been successfully reared or has suffered because no woman brought him up, and one may asume, as very probable, that Artie has flourished at least to the extent of not becoming a juvenile delinquent, or a jailbird. But this argument cuts both ways. If Artie has turned out well without a stepmother—and it is almost needless to add that a good many children and stepmothers do not get along very well—then Mr. Birnstengel's only explicit reason for seeking a wife and asking for Congressional aid in securing one is either groundless or has been slowly disappearing year by year.

I hope it is clear that I am in a state of genuine perplexity, whether or not the perplexity is justified. Indeed, my sense of my own shortcomings in various spheres has been such as to make me paraphrase various well-known proverbs and maxims: "Never make the same mistake more than five or six times," "A rolling stone gathers no remorse," and the like.

Clearly, however, the subject of marriage interests me very much, otherwise I would not have paid so much attention not only to Mr. Birnstengel, but for many years to the authors of various works which deal directly or indirectly with the subject of marriage. This is to say that I know very well that I am hardly the person to advise Mr. Birnstengel, particularly since I have not been asked for advice. However, I can speak with more assurance about the views of various illustrious authors who have written on the subject of marriage and whom Mr. Birnstengel, if he is like most of the farmers I have known, probably has not read. The chief justification, if there is any, for presuming to pass along a synopsis of these doctrines is that Mr. Birnstengel's categories are, at least as reported, somewhat narrow and limited unless I have misread the works of various authors, particularly Freud and Kierkegaard.

I mention these two because I admire their teachings very much and I am not alone: their doctrines have gained worldwide esteem. But I must admit some misgiving in commending and attempting an epitome of their views, a particular misgiving based upon a very slight knowledge of Mr. Artie Shaw, the jazz musician.

It may or may not be well-known that Mr. Artie Shaw as of this writing has been married eight times, that when his marriage to Miss Ava Gardner ended in divorce, that beautiful Hollywood star told the press that her marriage had been unhappy because her husband had insisted that she read the works of Freud and Kierkegaard. I hope it is not gratuitous to make explicit the moral which most husbands ought to draw from this instance, which is, never to insist that one's spouse read Freud and Kierkegaard, or like authors. It must also be said that Mr. Shaw is perhaps an ambiguous example: so I would suppose, at any rate, from the biographical entry about Mr. Shaw which I encountered in *Who's Who* while looking up some other celebrity. Mr. Shaw's biographical entry, which he almost certainly wrote himself, is unique: He lists all eight wives, and the list is certainly extremely impressive, including as it does Miss Ava Gardner, Miss Lana Turner, Miss Kathleen Winsor, among others.

A random sampling of other biographical entries made what I had suspected quite clear. Most of the human beings in *Who's Who* mentioned their wives only if they were still married to them, and there was a natural and understandable tendency to omit any mention of divorced wives or husbands. Mr. Shaw is equally understandable and natural in his explicit naming of all eight wives, which I think can rightly be interpreted as an expression of great pride. Mr. Shaw, like the rest of us, doubtless has his shortcomings, but any human being who can persuade so many beautiful and famous and sought-after women to marry him is justified in making his pride and his success explicit. I may be wrong, but I do not think that the same claim could be made for Mr. Tommy Manville, who has surpassed Mr. Shaw's record: The reason is that Mr. Manville's brides have not been courted, desired, and admired as much as some of Mr. Shaw's wives.

Mr. Shaw is, so far as a stranger can judge, the very antithesis of Mr. Birnstengel in regard to marriage. And if it must be admitted that Mr. Shaw may have been making too much of a good thing, nevertheless his example does suggest that Mr. Birnstengel's extreme circumspection is self-defeating, even if it is entirely correct to suppose that Mr. Birnstengel is far more interested in mail from unmarried females than in actually getting married. It is certainly not unjustifiable speculation to suppose that Mr. Shaw's fan mail has often been female, and that if he had made a public announcement of his desire to hear from candidates for his heart, he would have received more mail than Mr. Birnstengel at any time in the past fifteen years.

Let us consider the doctrines of Freud and Kierkegaard, both of whom, one may suppose, Mr. Shaw would agree possess a greater insight into the subject of marriage than he does. Freud and Kierkegaard, although their points of view and conclusions are very different, nevertheless are in unquestionable agreement about marriage: They both think that most human beings ought to get married. It is true that one of Freud's descriptions of the feminine character would scare the most courageous and lovelorn man, but what he says is supposed to be true *before* marriage. A happy marriage, according to Freud, often frees a lady of traits of character far worse than the faults which Mr. Birnstengel fears, and which may not be quite as serious as Mr. Birnstengel seems to think, to judge by his refusal of 8,000 applicants. To be churchy, a smoker, a drinker, too young or too old are characteristics and habits which would need not necessarily prevent a lady from being "Just Right." Moreover, Freud teaches that drinking and smoking as vices or excesses are often the result of a lady's unmarried condition and may very well be eliminated or diminished by a happy marriage, since they are very often the result of the nervousness and sense of being unloved which an unmarried female naturally feels. Love itself, according to Freud, is "the overestimation of the loved object," but although such a statement may seem to support Mr. Birnstengel's hesitation and delay, its real meaning, when one thinks about it sufficiently, is that Mr. Birnstengel, among other human beings, has been seeking an object to over-estimate.

I must admit Freud's views of marriage and of the feminine character cannot be reduced to a brief summary, and add that Freud's teachings about what he calls character formation traits might be of direct use to Mr. Birnstengel in extending his categories. Is such an extension desirable, however, now that the volume of mail has diminished so much? Surely the important point, whatever Mr. Birnstengel's essential aims may be, is to view marriage as a genuine and desirable possi-bility, however great the hazards. It is here that Freud and Kierkegaard concur. Kierkegaard is just as difficult to sum-marize as Freud, and he wrote about marriage at length and in detail, although often indirectly and often to justify his refusal to marry the woman he loved. Indeed the very title of one of his works on the subject is *Fear and Trembling*, which hardly sounds like a celebration of matrimony. But in this book and other like works, Kierkegaard's point is that one must make a choice and abide by it, in matrimony as in all things, in order to be a mature human being. Unless one takes a chance—or, to use Kierkegaard's phrase—makes "the leap into the absurd," a human being is merely a butterfly, a dilet-tante, an idler, a ne'er-do-well. What Kierkegaard regards as the absurdity of choice is, I think, identical with what Freud means when he speaks of "love's irrationality" and love as "an overestimation," although one might very well ask: "Who determines the correct estimation?" Or, "How or by what criterion is the correct estimation, which is neither an overestimation nor an underestimation, determined?"

The truth about love and marriage may be an eternal mystery despite all the discourse about it. This is certainly suggested by the well-known maxim that "marriages are made in heaven," the far less familiar statement that "marriage is the mystery of joy," and the obscure religious tradition that God, having too little to do after making Heaven and Earth in six days, decided on the eighth day that He henceforth would be a marriage broker. But although Mr. Birnstengel's fifteenth year of pursuit of the right bride gives rise—as I hardly need say at this point—to endless reflections, I am far less concerned with his interest in wedlock than with my own bewilderment, which is a new kind of bewilderment.

What I cannot understand and what makes me feel profoundly disturbed is not so much Mr. Birnstengel's problem and plight in itself—others have been and will be as critical and hesitant as he, just as others have been and will be impetuous and heedless—but the attitude of Mr. Birnstengel's Congressman, Mr. O'Konski and to a lesser extent the attitude of the Associated Press, other news services all around the world, and *The New York Times*, to say nothing of other persons and institutions who might have helped Mr. Birnstengel during the past fifteen years. After fifteen years and 8,000 letters, the farmer should have found a wife.

AN AUTHOR'S BROTHER-IN-LAW

Soon after getting married, my wife and I went to spend the summer on her father's farm. Her father was a very good painter and had lived upon this farm for the past fifteen summers, and here his son Claude lived with him too during the summer when school was over. I had only met Claude a few times before my wedding, but I regarded him as precisely what one would desire in a young brother-in-law, if one had much choice in such matters. I felt that I had acquired not only a very fine brother-in-law, but one who was just the right age. This feeling may or may not be common among happy bridegrooms: My only information on the subject derived from memories of comic strips of twenty-five and thirty years prior to the present—comic strips in which the kid has to be bribed throughout the courtship to depart from the scene of the necking, which cannot make for very good relations after the marriage, particularly since the kid is likely to think he can continue getting paid at the same rate, under entirely different circumstances. In any case, I had had no such problems since Claude was not present prior to my marriage. In addition to all this suggestion of a fortunate future, I had been very fond of my younger brother throughout childhood and youth, so I would suppose, looking back, that I really yearned for a renewal of that happy personal relationship.

When the happy bridegroom and bride arrived in a recently purchased jalopy, nine-year-old Claude, always shy, seemed shyer than before. We came, bearing gifts and the gift for Claude was a cold boiled lobster, something which Claude, I knew, regarded as far superior to the treasures contained at Fort Knox. But Claude appeared to be less interested in the lobster than in the old car. I immediately promised to turn it over to him when he reached sixteen. This was a fairly safe promise to make to a boy of nine, but since he was well aware of the length of time and since the old age of the jalopy was obvious, I made haste to add that it might not be running by that time, seven years hence.

"I'll get it to run if it's not running," Claude said then, losing all his shyness and getting into the front seat. It took me a few minutes to perceive that the ancient vehicle was, from Claude's point of view, far superior to a Rolls-Royce since it would enable him to qualify for membership in the hot-rod set.

The day after, my wife and I settled ourselves in the log cabin which was to be our domicile for the summer and which was a hundred yards away from the farmhouse where Claude and his father lived, and late in the afternoon Claude and I went swimming in the old rock quarry pool. We reached the quarry by walking down along an old Indian path, and as we went there, Claude announced with family and personal pride that the quarry belonged to him because it was part of his father's property. It was while we were swimming that the first sign of trouble set in, for I found a turtle and put it on the rocks and Claude insisted that I throw it back because his father had told him that the pool needed turtles. The insistence was astonishing from so polite and tactful a boy as Claude. But bygones seemed to have gone by by the time we had had dinner, and I invited Claude to accompany me to the village for an ice cream soda. He accepted the invitation, stipulating, however, that he be permitted to ride in the rumble seat of the old coupe. This request seemed natural enough until, as we set out and I put the car in gear, Claude pulled down the rumble seat hood and sat down, with a thump upon the rumble seat floor which thus made the rumble seat his personal subway for a mile and a half. When we arrived in the village, Claude emerged from his cave, looking a little dazed as blinking audiences do coming out of the moving pictures after three hours of Hollywood moonlight. He made no comment, but led me to the ice cream parlor, seated himself upon a stool, and soon was sucking away through a straw at his black-and-white ice cream soda, wearing a look of devout and concentrated pleasure. I surprised myself by wanting a second ice cream soda and Claude surprised me by wanting one also. We left soon after in mutual silence. Claude was pensive as he returned to his mobile catacomb, shaking his head as he refused my offer of a Pogo book if he would consent to ride next to me in the suicide seat.

More trouble of a more serious kind began the next afternoon when we went swimming again and Claude's father came along. Claude and his father had always been very devoted to one another, but after diving in the pool and climbing up the rock face, Claude expressed an open unprovoked and unprecedented antagonism towards his father.

"You're just an old fuddy-duddy!" said Claude. He added several more simple characterizations in the very same polemical style, to which his father did not respond. I was foolish enough to try to stop Claude by promising to tell him a story, but he refused to be diverted.

"Tonight, after supper, I might, if I feel like it," said Claude, hurling another remark at his father and diving back into the pool when he saw no response upon his father's face.

Before dinner my wife, who saw that I was disappointed, told me that she thought Claude was angry at his father because his father and mother had been divorced during the year, his mother had married again, and Claude, loving both his father and mother and regarding his father as the stronger by far of the two, blamed his father for the separation, the divorce, and his mother's remarriage, believing that none of these events would have occurred if his powerful father had truly wished to prevent them. Claude credited his father with an omnipotence which he himself expected one day to possess.

This explanation, whether true or false, was comforting, and it was even more comforting when at dinner time domestic tranquility was again disturbed by Claude's profound animus and disappointment.

"You're an old fuddy-duddy too," he said to me suddenly out of a clear but darkening sky. "I don't want to hear any of your old stories, you old fuddy-duddy." He relented to the extent, however, of accepting my invitation to the village drug store two hours later. For the second night in succession I had a second soda and invited Claude to have two sodas also, which he did, expressing his gratitude—or so I supposed—by saying that he would like to hear a story about the olden times, but not about when I was a boy. With little hesitation, I proceeded to tell him, as we drove home, a new version of the world famous story of William Tell. Claude had heard various versions at various times, partly perhaps because his father was partly Swiss, partly French, and entirely American. As a result of these previous versions Claude kept correcting me and contradicting me about one detail after another. But I had finished the entire story by the time we were driving up the hill which led to his father's farmhouse: I then asked him a question which had occurred to me while telling the story: "Who was the real hero of the story of William Tell, the father or the son?"

"Everyone knows that William Tell was the hero, everyone knows that," Claude said scornfully.

"He was the hero before and after the apple episode, but the real hero when William Tell shot the arrow at his son's head was the son."

"Everyone says that the father is the hero all through," Claude said stubbornly. "I suppose you know the story better than anybody else," he added ironically.

"Never mind me: Don't you think that the son had to be even more courageous than his father when he stood still with an apple on his head and his father shooting at him? I guess maybe we better agree that the father and the son were both heroes," I said, supposing that perhaps Claude had been attempting to defend his father from the slings and arrows of outraged matrimony.

"Someone would have thought of that long before you did if it were true," said Claude pensively.

I had parked the car on the lawn and Claude left me without further comment, departing for his cavelike bedroom.

Before continuing with this account I had better say something about myself, as an author, attempting once again to speak of my profession and my own work without winning, as I have before, the Silver Trophy for Conspicuous Modesty. I had published three volumes of poetry and one book of stories. I had been praised a good deal, particularly for my first book of poems and for my book of fiction, suffering, as is natural, the customary rush of blood and *hubris* to the head. I had also grown accustomed to being told by most people that they did not understand my modern poetry. Thus when I sent my younger brother a copy of my first book of poems he acknowledged it with his customary candor: He was pleased to get the book and he liked it very much except that he did not like poetry; and he had shown the book to his friends—this was during the last year of the Great Depression—and his friends had been sufficiently impressed to say that they would certainly buy a copy if they had the $2.50. I had had many other experiences of the same kind subsequently, such as invitations to dinner and to weekends. All of them made me aware that although people did not understand modern poetry they were overjoyed to entertain a modern poet. During the previous summer my book of fiction appeared and was reviewed with extreme generosity in a national periodical known for the severity of its book reviews. For a brief period I had lost my sense of proportion: The national weekly had at that time a circulation of more than three million readers which made me calculate as follows: If only one percent of the more than three million readers of the national weekly bought a copy of my book—this seemed to me, in my then emotional state, not an unreasonable expectation—my publisher would love me very much and my bank account would grow like a green bay tree. (I had been trying to buy a second-hand green bay tree for several years.) A year after, I learned how wrong I was. The three million

readers of the national weekly did not all read the book reviews in it and those who did read the reviews did so in order
to be able not to have to buy and read the book. This explanation explained everything to me: It also explained how naive
it is possible for an author to be for I had until then assumed
that the purpose of a book review was to advise the reader as
to whether a book was worth reading, and it had never occurred to me that book reviews might be written week after
week chiefly in order to make the reading of books unnecessary. At this point I realized my own guilt also, for I too had
been reading book reviews in order to avoid reading a good
many books.

The relevance of this information to my blossoming friendship with my newly acquired brother-in-law will be apparent
as soon as possible. Our nightly excursions to the village drug
store soon stopped. I no longer wanted two sodas an evening,
although Claude did. I no longer wanted even one soda after
dinner. Claude was perplexed and irritated. I was perplexed
also. Then I realized how the intuitive wisdom of the body
had been at work. I had stopped drinking all alcoholic bever-
ages abruptly upon arriving at the farm, and this abrupt ces-
sation, after the inundation of the cocktail parties of the
previous spring, had left my wise interior in a state of extreme deprivation, clamoring for sugar, and willing to accept
what the ice cream parlor provided for lack of the quicker
abundance to which it had been so recently accustomed.
Clearly this explanation could not be communicated to Claude
for at least ten years to come, and the one bond between us,
ice cream sodas, was severed. I offered to finance him on a
lend-lease basis but he refused and made it clear that I was
just letting him down, for to offer him the wherewithal to

buy ice cream sodas was hardly the same thing as being my ice-cream-soda-drinking companion. It was a handout and hence unacceptable since he was not a beggar and this was neither his birthday nor Christmas.

Thus Claude had a new and very good reason for being a harsh critic not only of fathers and family life, but poets, storytellers and brothers-in-law.

One afternoon during this period of disaffection and misunderstanding, he came calling upon me to suggest that I get a well-paying job. I usually sat all day long in a beach chair in front of the cabin with books, papers, notebooks, typewriter, and writing board nearby; and to an uninformed observer it certainly would have seemed that most of the time I was doing very little except attempting to acquire a suntan. The truth is that I was not feeling very productive and could hardly have convinced myself that I was doing much work unless brooding about my relationship with my brother-in-law can be characterized as gainful employment: Most of the time I was self-unemployed.

"Why don't you get a job at the country club as a caddy?" Claude asked me, and he looked genuinely concerned about his brother-in-law's income. "You'd make a lot of money, you might get big tips sometimes, you'd get more exercise, and you'd get to know a lot of very nice people."

"I do all right now," I said, perplexed. "Nothing sensational, but I make enough to keep your sister and myself well fed and I can even buy you a soda now and then."

"Don't you want more money than you have?" Claude inquired, also perplexed.

"Sure I want more money than I have, but I don't want to do all of the things I would have to do to make more money than I do make. For example, if I became a golf caddy I might make more money, but I would have less time to write poems and stories."

This made no sense to Claude, so I tried to compare myself to the hunters and fishermen and guides explaining that some of them might prefer to be guides at a comparatively low rate of pay doing what they liked to do rather than work at jobs in the city which made more money. But Claude looked perplexed again. That evening my wife said that the reason surely for his perplexity was that hunting and fishing were fun, while my apparent idleness all day long, sitting in the sunlight, reading and writing in one or another notebook, was not Claude's idea of fun. It was like schoolwork and I was no longer a schoolboy.

Claude renewed his suggestion the next day, offering to help by selling the lost golf balls I would probably find while caddying.

"Why don't you be a caddy if you think it's such a good job, Claude?" I said to him, fearing again that I might be taking him too seriously.

"I'm too young," he said, looking pensive.

Instead of answering more directly, he suggested new roads to wealth—the giveaway programs on the radio and, in the spring, a job as an usher at Madison Square Garden when the circus came to town, and when I refused to entertain these proposals, he said that I'd be sorry. "T.S. on you," he remarked, then and for several weeks more, the initials meaning Tough Situation, although for some time I supposed them to be an esoteric and ironic reference to that very great poet T.S. Eliot.

In midsummer, the FCC banned giveaway programs, and I showed the newspaper headlines to Claude in triumph. But soon after, the principal of his school won a Buick in a lottery of some sort and Claude came to me with the news and added that the principal not only knew more than I did, but could write better poems than I wrote if he wanted to do so.

"How do you know? Has he?" I asked, and suggested that he ask the principal if he had the same opinion.

"He has four children," said Claude. And if I had not been amazed by this rejoinder, I might have been indiscreet enough to remark that his sister and I had been married too short a time to have any children. The best I could say was that I had to admit that a man who had four children had my respect and esteem and I might think of him as a person worthy of emulation.

"Big words: You always use big words," said Claude. "Emulation!"

I explained what the word meant and Claude said that if that's all that emulation meant why did I have to use a big word instead of the small ones that everyone used. He departed before I answered since he was entertaining his friends at the quarry.

Several days later, at breakfast, Claude brought the mail in and it contained an anthology which not only had several of my poems, but my photograph also. Claude glanced at the photograph and I told him that it had been taken eleven years before and that it was the work of a photographer for one of the fashion magazines which specialized in glamorizing the person photographed.

"I don't look like that now, I know," I said, "and I did not look like that then either."

"Oh, you do, a little," Claude said, and if I had been more perceptive I would have understood that a turning point in our friendship had been reached. For there was a real intention of kindness in his remark, and, according to my wife, who was silently regarding us and drinking her breakfast coffee, Claude, whom she knew well, probably thought that I felt sad about my age, since at thirty-five I seemed to Claude, at nine, to have been born early in the eighteenth century.

"I would rather be the age I am now, Claude, than the age I was eleven years ago," I said, and was about to continue with remarks about how pleased I was to be thirty-five and not twenty-four and miserable, but then, just in time, I realized that this would be entirely meaningless to Claude even when he was twenty-four.

A few days later, the mail again brought me an unexpected letter from a boy of sixteen—the age of reason, manhood, and the hot-rod set to Claude. This letter contained a request for my autograph and a sentence which referred to my photograph in the recently published anthology: If I looked as kind as my photograph seemed to suggest, then I would surely be generous enough to grant the writer's request. It was obvious to me, on the basis of many other like requests, that my correspondent was engaged in autograph-collecting, an activity isolated from all other things just as stamp-collecting and coin-collecting are. The request had no relation whatever to the reading of anything in print. I handed the letter to Claude and made no comment, departing for my daily station in the sun near the cabin. No sooner had I established myself in my deck chair, where I could be a wise guy without irritating anyone but myself, than Claude appeared.

"What are you going to do about that guy who wants your autograph?" Claude asked me eagerly.

"What do you think I should do?" I answered cautiously. "Why don't you act as my advisor—what would you do if you were me?"

The Ego Is Always at the Wheel

Claude thought for a while, stared at me, and then advised me to give the autograph to the autograph-collector. "Give the guy a break," said Claude judiciously.

I answered by saying that it was very doubtful that my correspondent read what I wrote—he was too busy with his hobby to have the time. Claude replied, more judicious than ever, that some day the autograph-collector might, but he might not if I did not give him what he wanted now.

In the evening, I was told that Claude had asked his father whether the letter was bona fide or a put-up job. He had done so in the brief interval between my departure from the breakfast table and his arrival to discuss the request with me.

Claude had learned all about being suspicious and all about being important at the moon-pictures, but nevertheless his inquiry was inspired by a personal feeling: He had a low opinion of me and was suspicious of me because he did not think I was the kind of a fellow who would be asked for his autograph but he did think, on the basis of the ice cream sodas, for example, that I was certainly the kind of fellow who would stop at nothing in order to impress him and writing myself a favorable poison-pen letter was precisely the kind of a thing he expected me to do from time to time.

A new era of intimacy now began as I discovered the next morning when Claude appeared at the breakfast table and said that he wanted to see me about something very special, so would I meet him in his hideout, a tent behind the quarry, and a sacred spot: I had never been invited there before, although Claude met his friends there very often and sometimes camped out with them in the tent on very hot nights.

When I arrived at this sanctuary an hour after being invited, Claude was there, waiting for me, and holding his stamp-collection in his right hand.

"You can have any one you want in exchange," he said looking nervous. I suppose he thought I might drive a hard bargain.

"In exchange for what?" I naturally wanted to know.

"In exchange for your autograph of course!" said Claude, astonished by my ignorance and by my lack of desire for any of his stamps.

With more tact than I commonly command I refused to accept any of his stamps, yet refrained from expressing any lack of desire for them. I pointed out that, as his brother-in-law, I was not in a position to accept payment and besides his sister and I were living for nothing on his father's farm which would one day be his.

This was not so much a happy ending as a happy beginning. The following April Claude and his sister accompanied me to the opening game of the National League race at the Polo Grounds. Claude was aware that I had been a fanatic Giant fan since John McGraw's eminence as a mastermind and since the time when Casey Stengel played centerfield for the Giants and beat the Yankees in two games of the World Series by hitting home runs within the park and beating the throw to the catcher by exertions which made him look like a famished otter. The Giants lost the opening game and Claude, recognizing how sorrowful this defeat left me, announced as we mounted Coogan's Bluff, that family loyalty and solidarity made it necessary for him to become a Giant rooter, like myself, even though the Giants were no good and he had been a Dodger fan until then. He explained to me that I had been a Giant rooter far, far longer than he had been a Dodger rooter and the entire matter was too crucial and too important to permit of any family dissension.

"We have to stick together," he said with the dignity reserved for all matters of loyalty. Reflecting upon his new allegiance I silently congratulated him on his wisdom: The sort of hatred which existed of necessity between Giant fans and Dodger fans would hardly be desirable within the family. My wife, however, knows both of us better than we know each other or ourselves: She thought at the time, and told me, that the crucial reason for so drastic a change of heart on Claude's part was a very different one. Claude had decided, possessed by the kind of intuition which guides Willie Mays when he goes after a long fly, that he was more likely to get to go to the Polo Grounds than to Ebbets Field as long as I was his brother-in-law, and if this fair and reasonable expectation proved true, he would obviously have to become a Giant fan. Otherwise, he would be faced with an unbearable and heartbreaking dilemma or trilemma. He would have to be disloyal to the Dodgers at the Polo Grounds or refuse to go to the Polo Grounds except when the Dodgers were there or—worst of all—he would have to become the kind of mad dog who goes to the Polo Grounds only to see the Giants lose. In other words, a Yankee fan.

THE DIFFICULTY OF DIVORCE

It was very nice of the Princess Elizabeth to say something about the problem of marriage and divorce in the modern world. Obviously she had no direct personal stake or bias, because *she* is not going to get a divorce, not after what happened to her Uncle Ed when he wanted to marry a divorced woman: The British Empire will not survive another constitutional crisis like that, no matter how powerful the R. A. F., for though war is worse than divorce, the latter tends to undermine morale. And if we might tend to suppose that Elizabeth did not at the age of twenty-two have enough experience either in her own life or through observation of her friends' alliances to discuss these things, nevertheless you can be a good tennis coach, even if you are not a tennis star, so I guess even if you have only been married once and intend to continue, you probably have some sensible points to contribute to the discussion. Anyway, if you are going to be Queen of England, you just have to have decided opinions about practically everything, even if it's only the press agent's prejudices.

The Ego Is Always at the Wheel

Yet I wonder what the future Queen would have to say about the experience of a friend of mine in trying to get a divorce? This friend of mine and his wife had decided to get a divorce because they liked each other very much, but not enough. My friend's wife liked my friend very much, but was unable to get over the fact that he did not resemble Gary Cooper in the least. For one thing, he talked too much while Cooper, as is well known, is very reticent and at times seems to be tongue-tied. (This lady also liked Conrad Veidt the German film star until the day of his death, and this posed a problem because Veidt also talked a great deal, like her husband, but he spoke with a charming continental accent which made all the difference in the world.)

Well, anyway, when this friend of mine and his wife had decided to get a divorce, they discovered that in the state of New York it was very difficult to get one unless the husband committed bona fide adultery. If it was not bona fide, then the judge might get sore, throw the case out of court, and make it impossible for either of the two ever to get a divorce at all, at least in New York. Now my friend was not very much against committing adultery, but he did not like the idea of committing it in cold blood. It reminded him of eating when not hungry. However, his wife's lawyer advised her that this was necessary, and he was insistent. He urged that certain precautions be taken. It was dangerous, he told her, telling her to tell her husband, for her husband to pick up a blonde in a bar, because she might later blackmail him and say that he had not committed bona fide adultery with her. My friend, hearing this, was very much distressed, because he felt that he just could not ask any other lady he knew to make believe that she was committing adultery with him. It was one thing to get some lady friend to commit adultery. That might take some persuasion but at least it was not insincere and insulting. However, it was something else again to get some friend merely to put in an appearance in a hotel bedroom. She might be very much insulted and offended by the suggestion, which would not make her out to be very attractive, when you consider its implications, I mean the implications of such a proposal. On the other hand, if one did commit adultery, it would be extremely awkward to say the least, to plan to have one's wife come barging in with two witnesses, who, as the lawyer insisted, had to be friends of both. My friend felt that if he went through with a disingenuous performance such as seemed to be necessary, then word might get about that he was merely using his female friends in order to solve and circumvent certain legal difficulties. Besides, he was shy, and he did not want anyone knocking on the hotel door and entering while he and a lady were in a state of disarray, undress, and distress.

He discussed the problem with his former-wife-to-be at dinner and she agreed that it was very difficult for him and that he must try to avoid any of the implications of disrespect to his lady friends by proposing that they join with him in this unflattering farce.

After dinner, they joined a married couple who had already consented to be witnesses of my friend's false adultery, and the married couple agreed that there were obvious dangers involved and they sat about in a bar and tried to solve their problem, but they did not seem to be getting anywhere until my friend had what seemed to him a wonderful idea: His wife would commit adultery with him! She would be her own co-respondent. They would go, all four, to his hotel suite and she would go to the bedroom, take off her dress, move from the bedroom to the bathroom when the married couple knocked on the door, and being seen in her slip by them as she passed from the bedroom to the bathroom, she might be identified in court as being a woman in a state of undress in my friend's bedroom. What judge in a thousand years would ask the married couple who were going to testify against my friend if they were sure that the woman in undress was not my friend's wife? It just would not occur to any judge. My friend was also delighted by the idea because, just as it seemed to involve no falsification of the truth, so too, in his wife's being her own corespondent, there was a theological parallel he liked very much. It was just like the Father, the Son, and the Holy Ghost!

His wife and the married couple were not as enchanted by this project as he was, but after further discussion, there did not seem anything else to do (except to pick up a blonde and risk blackmail), so they decided to go through with the whole thing, and they did, and they were very nervous and they made nervous jokes such as "who was the corespondent I saw you with in the bedroom?" "That was no corespondent, that was my former wife," but everything turned out very well and at the trial the judge did not ask the testifying witness any simple and direct questions and the divorce was granted, but the wife and the married couple grew very nervous anyway because they thought the scheme was too clever and after the trial they went out to a bar to get a few quick ones because they all had a guilty conscience.

What would the Princess Elizabeth have to say about this ordeal? Would she not have to agree that a divorce, of course, ought not to be made so difficult and should not make necessary so much falsehood or bona fide adultery? As the divorce laws now stand in the State of New York and in England, I believe, there is implicit in them an open invitation to immorality, if anyone who is sensitive wants to avoid insincerity, perjury, disingenuity, and insults to members of the opposite sex. Of course, her main point was that people ought not to get divorced at all, but since this would only lead to more and more adultery, judging by the facts, she would be caught on the horns of a dilemma.

However, it must be admitted that of late divorce too has become very peculiar. People not only take marriage lightly, they also seem to be incapable of taking a divorce very seriously. For example, two, not only one, of my acquaintances, have shown a tendency to visit their former wives after the divorce has gone through and to spend the night with them. One of them explained to me that after you have been married for a long time, you form certain habits which tend to continue in spite of the fact that you have been divorced, which tends to seem somewhat of a legal abstraction, especially since you get along so well with your former wife when the chief obstacle to getting along with her, marriage, has been removed. The other acquaintance who was a victim of this habit was very shamefaced about it, however. He claimed that he had stayed overnight because he could not get a room in a hotel and matters had gone much further than he had expected because it was a winter night and his former wife's apartment was poorly heated by her infamous landlord.

If anyone thinks I am being frivolous or just talking through my hat on this subject, they are wrong. I have studied it very carefully, from the point of view of immediate personal experience, from the judicious and calm point of view of an observer concerned about the vicissitudes of his friends' marriages, and have taken what I think I may say without immodesty is a scholarly approach. As to personal experience, that is one thing, but what I really take a great deal of pride in is my learning on the subject of marriage. I am not thinking only of all the motion pictures and plays and novels to which I have devoted myself and which for the most part circled about the question of marriage, whether it was *Anna Karenina, Oedipus Rex, Gone With the Wind, Tobacco Road,* or *Abie's Irish Rose.* I am also thinking of what has happened to *The Book of Common Prayer,* a work which is very influential indeed and in the English-speaking world provides the model for all marriage ceremonies, for even if you are not a communicant of a church which uses *The Book of Common Prayer,* it is extremely unlikely that you do not go to the motion pictures where, needless to say, you must have encountered the use of the Anglican marriage service more than once and found it very beautiful.

It is very beautiful. But it has been tampered with, and in an unfortunate way, by prudes, I suspect, who have no real feeling for the sacrament of marriage or the beauty of human relationships.

Thus nowadays, at the moment when the groom places the ring upon the bride's hand, the fair bride says: "With this ring I thee wed, with my body I thee worship, with all my worldly goods I thee endow."

How that phrase, "with my body I thee worship," survived, amid other expurgations, is a perplexing matter: Probably carelessness. For just look what has happened elsewhere. At a previous moment in the ceremony, the minister asks the bride the following familiar question: "Wilt thou have this man to thy wedded husband, to live together after God's holy ordinance in the holy estate of matrimony? Wilt thou obey him, and serve him, love, honour, and keep him in sickness and in health; and forsaking all others, keep thee only unto him, so long as ye both shall live?" Nowadays, the bride just says that she will do all these things. In the old days before the ceremony was revised, the bride used to have to say: "I take thee to my weddyd husbonde to haue and to holde fro thys day for bether, for wurs, for richer, for porer, in sykeness and hin elthe to be bonour and buxom in bed and at bort tyll deth do us departe yf holy chyrche wol it ordeyne: and ther to I plyche te my throute."

Now this is certainly a far cry from what is pledged today. My edition of *The Book of Common Prayer* has a commentary in it written by some Victorian named Blunt (God save the mark!) in 1883 and he shows that he is quite disturbed by the old form of the ceremony, even though it was by then long since not in style. He explains that "Bonour and buxom" are the representatives of "Bonnaire," gentle (as in *débonnaire*) and "Boughsome," obedient. But that's just silly, as you can see if you look again and regard the context. The bride says that she is going to be bonour and buxom in bed and at board. How can you be gentle at board? Perhaps the pious Victorian is thinking of good manners at the dinner table, but it is not very likely that that's what the authors of the ceremony were thinking about because they had a very different idea of good manners. And for that matter to be obedient in bed does not strike me as being a very cogent promise, though being buxom and *débonnaire* seems quite sensible, but I don't want to go into unnecessary detail. My main point is that this illustrates how people have not been paying the proper attention to marriage, and how the institution as a whole is in a parlous state, just as is this profound and beautiful ceremony, which has been spoiled by revision, weakened, and (I believe it is not too much to say) emasculated.

This brings us back to the Princess Elizabeth. If she is really concerned about matrimony today, let her consider these facts and in particular the degradation of the marriage ceremony. One of these days she will be the secular head of the Church of England, and it will then be possible for her to do something about the whole affair in this very important matter of what is said at the very start of the marriage by the bride to the groom in the presence of witness, friends, and relatives. Who knows what may not come of this?

POSTSCRIPT: A friend of mine married his true love recently, after an arduous courtship full of much misunderstanding. He and his beautiful bride embraced matrimony only after both had often visited psychoanalysts who helped them to understand themselves and each other. The joyous pair sent me the following wedding card:

Dr. Martin Green & Dr. Theodore Burns
announce the marriage of their well-meaning patients
Miss Isabel Basel Doolittle & Mr. Bertram Y. Kennedy

Love is no longer blind! It's a wise man who knows his wife or for that matter himself:
Ah, Psyche from the regions which
Are Holy Land!

THE FAMOUS ELEPHANT

"We will find out about life through this elephant!" said the seven blind men. The first one touched him, feeling his trunk.

"He is a rope or a lasso," said the first blind man.

The second blind man touched his legs, first the front leg then the hind leg.

"You are wrong. He is a pillar or a column. I made sure by touching him in two different places, far apart," said the second blind man.

The third blind man brushed his hands along the width of the elephant's body.

"You are both wrong. Neither of you examined him well. He is like the side of a mountain, long and wide. I know, because I touched him from one end to the other," said the third blind man.

The fourth blind man touched the genitals of the elephant, and they arose.

"He is a powerful snake, first limp and then stiff as a rod, and coiled," cried the fourth blind man.

The fifth blind man said, "Let us not dispute with each other. It must be that you are right—he is a rope, a pillar, the side of a mountain, and a powerful snake. He is all these things." And he touched the elephant in several parts and then he was sure that to add the parts was to come to the truth.

"You are all wrong," cried the sixth blind man. "All of you say a different thing of the elephant, and each cannot be right, because no thing can be a powerful snake and the side of a mountain at the same time." Then he touched the worst part of the elephant and cried in anguish, "He is filthy and evil."

"We cannot know what he is, our senses cannot reach him, but he knows himself what he is, for he is himself, he is in himself: Perhaps if we asked him, he would tell us what he is?" said the seventh.

So they asked him and the elephant bellowed loudly and without meaning: A roar, an uproar, a sound like the cracking of ice and then like the roar of coal down a chute, and then like an organ erupting, Vesuvian.

"Agh, brek-ke-ko-ax, agh, awe, ah!" roared the elephant. "Hemt-on-timor-menus!"

And the seven blind men said in chorus that the elephant was a darkness of fearful and incoherent sound. He was an immense thunder. He was a rush of cacophonous chaos, and they withdrew as the elephant moved, and they were afraid, and they began to run.

HAMLET, OR THERE IS SOMETHING WRONG WITH EVERYONE

Hamlet came from an old upper-class family. He was the only son of a king. He was very intelligent, though somewhat of an intellectual, and he was quite handsome too, except for a tendency to get fat in the face and thicken. The Prime Minister Polonius itched with an eagerness to get Hamlet to marry his beautiful, charming, and sweet-tempered daughter Ophelia. Not only that, but more important by far, Ophelia was very much in love with Hamlet, and when Hamlet went to Germany to study metaphysics and lager beer, she thought about him all the time. "That's what love or infatuation seems to me," said Ophelia. "It's when you think of someone all the time, wondering what the loved one is thinking, what he is doing, and if he will ever love you the way you love him," which is not very likely, most things tending to be one-sided affairs.

Hamlet's father, the king, died suddenly, and right after the funeral, Hamlet's mother remarried, her new husband being Claudius, the king's brother who now became king himself.

The Ego Is Always at the Wheel

The marriage took place very soon after the funeral and Hamlet was enraged and it was then that Hamlet began to behave in a most peculiar manner much to everyone's surprise and perplexity. He had always been very careful about his appearance, even somewhat of a dandy: Now he looked like someone who has slept for three nights in a railroad coach, and slept very poorly at that. He had always been consistently sensible, polite, and full of tact. Now he made all kinds of remarks which no one could understand, and he went about looking very glum, but it was better when he was glum because when he opened his mouth, he said something which seemed, at best, mysterious, and often enough, maniacal. For example, when his mother said that he ought not to be so sad about his father's death, because the show must go on, life is full of inevitable losses, everyone is bound to die, sooner or later, what did Hamlet say in answer? He requested his mother to sing for him as she had when he was a child, the old songs "My Old Kentucky Womb," and "Carry Me Back To Old Virginity." Naturally she did not know what to make of this.

Some people thought that he was behaving like that because he was very much in love with Ophelia. But that's ridiculous. Ophelia would have married him without hesitation. And even those who thought that he was just a lovesick young man were not sure of this explanation and went about eavesdropping and looking through transoms each time Hamlet and Ophelia were alone with each other.

Other people, particularly Claudius his uncle the new king, thought that Hamlet was very angry because he wanted to be king himself. Claudius thought that everyone was just like he was, for he had wanted to be king very much.

The truth is that Hamlet did not care about being king because he was very depressed about everything. He just felt rotten, no matter what he did. And when he talked to his best friend Horatio, or visited with his old friend the local undertaker, what he talked about in the main was how depressed he was, how meaningless life seemed to him, and how he would like to commit suicide.

"There's an eternity that mocks our hopes," he said one day to Horatio, "no matter what we try." This was supposed to explain why he did not commit suicide, even though he felt like it. Horatio was polite, so he did not tell Hamlet that he did not understand a word of what he was saying.

Some people supposed that his mother's second marriage, and right after the funeral of his father, was what upset Hamlet so much. It is certainly true that Hamlet did behave in an extraordinary and offensive way with his mother, telling her that she had married too soon, that her new husband (and his uncle) was far from being as fine a man as his father had been, and that she ought not to let her new husband make love to her, among other ridiculous suggestions. According to this view of his conduct, he was jealous of his uncle and in love with his mother, who was still a very attractive woman.

There may be a great deal of truth in this view of Hamlet's behavior, for all we know, but then again how about his father? He never behaved like that when his father was alive, nor did he carry on in a sullen and disgruntled manner, not even as an infant. Still and all, this may be a superficial difficulty in observing Hamlet's true state of mind, for he was certainly horrified by the very idea of his uncle just touching his mother.

He said to her in fury one night in her bedroom,

The Ego Is Always at the Wheel

—to live,
In the rank sweat of an enseaméd bed,
Stewed in corruption, honeying, and making love
Over the nasty sty.

And many more remarks of the same kind, just as adolescent and irritating, indicating that he had a distinct aversion, to say the least, to the idea of people making love. Love seems to have been something dirty to him, in fact, a four letter word: L-O-V-E.

But something more than this incestuous jealousy was wrong with Hamlet, as you can see when you know that he told the sweet and likable Ophelia to become a nun. It's one thing to turn a girl down, but to make these proposals about her future, a future with which you refused to have anything to do, is quite insulting and shows how disgusted Hamlet was with the idea of anyone making love to anyone else. Probably he wanted Ophelia to become a nun so that no one would ever make love to her. And Horatio, who was a kind and well-meaning fellow, as well as a good friend, said to Hamlet that he had been very cruel to Ophelia and that he ought not to mistreat a girl just because she was very much in love with him.

"A pretty girl is like a canteloupe," replied Hamlet, "once opened, it begins to get rotten." What kind of a remark was that for a well-bred young man to make?

Horatio just sighed when he heard such things, for he realized that his friend was under a severe emotional strain.

"You never step twice into the same girl, as Heraclitus should have said," Hamlet continued, now that he was on the subject of girls. "I would like something more permanent."

"You did not always feel like this," Horatio remarked, "perhaps this is just a passing phase?"

Hamlet shrugged his shoulders and expressed contempt for his uncle the king on the ground that he drank too much.

"Those whom the gods would destroy, they first make successful," said Hamlet, apropos of nothing at all and at the same time everything, including his uncle's success and alcoholism, for he had become more and more given to statements of a quasi-philosophical and invariably cynical character.

"You better watch those human relationships," said Horatio, thinking again of how cruel Hamlet had been to Ophelia.

"That's what upset me so much," Hamlet fatuously replied, "I've been watching those human relationships, and I do not like them very much."

You can also see how sick a young man he was when you remember how beautiful, lovable, and delightful a creature Ophelia was. She would have done anything to make Hamlet happy. The fact that she was in love with him made absolutely no impact on him, except perhaps to irritate him because it was a distraction from what really preoccupied him.

"I had not thought life had undone so many," said Hamlet to Horatio and to Ophelia, in passing.

Some people also thought that Hamlet suspected his uncle of killing his father in order to get his throne and his wife, and consequently the reason that he felt badly and behaved strangely was that he felt that he ought to avenge his father's murder but suffered from a lack of will-power. But he did not suffer from lack of will-power, nor was he a coward, as some have supposed. This should be obvious because when he was sent to England by his uncle, ostensibly for a change of scene to improve his health and emotions, and when he found out that this trip was really a plot to get him killed in England, he acted swiftly, bravely, and with resolution, stealing the secret papers which contained orders to have him killed and fixing it so that his accompanists, who were in the pay of his uncle, would be wiped out instead of him: *Hardly* the behavior of a coward with no will-power!

It's true that he was disturbed by his father's death and detested his uncle but this hardly explains his state of mind, and he killed a man suddenly because he was eavesdropping behind the curtain when he was talking to his mother. He thought the spy was his uncle, but it was Ophelia's father, poor Polonius. Ophelia went insane quite reasonably because the man she loved had killed her father and she was in an inexorable emotional trap, from which she fled by means of drowning herself, an event which brought her brother back from his studies in France to challenge Hamlet to a duel. But as a result of tricky and despicable Claudius' machinations, this duel resulted in a virtual holocaust: Everyone was stabbed or poisoned to death, except Horatio.

People have been arguing for hundreds of years about what was really wrong with Hamlet. Some say that he must have been a woman, some say that he was homosexual, in love with his uncle or with Horatio, and unable to bear the fact that his uncle slept with a woman, and there is one fascinating view which maintains that all the mystery is utterly clarified if we suppose that everyone is roaring drunk from the beginning to the end of the play. This view is very fine except that I don't see how it clarifies anything, for drunk or sober, not everyone behaves the same, and the real question is why Hamlet behaved as he did: certainly just hitting the bottle does not account for all his emotions and opinions, and *in vino veritas*, anyway.

Needless to say, I have a theory too; in fact, several. But I don't know if it is correct or not. For if after all these years no one has explained why Hamlet felt as he did, it does not seem very likely that I can. However, for what it is worth, and to use clinical terms, I will say in brief that I think Hamlet suffered from a well-known pathological disorder. He was manic; and he was depressive. No one knows what the real causes of the manic-depressive disorder are, whether physical or mental or both, and that is why no one understands Hamlet.

Now that is my point, the fact that you can have this gift or that disease, and no one understands why, no one is responsible, and no one can really alter matters, and yet no one can stop thinking that someone is to blame. To be manic-depressive is just like being small or tall, strong, blond, fat— there is no clear reason for it, it is quite arbitrary, no one seems to have had any choice in the matter, and it is very important, certainly it is very important. This is the reason that the story of Hamlet is very sad, bad, and immoral. It has all these traits because Hamlet's diseased emotions caused the deaths of the beautiful Ophelia, her pompous but well-meaning father, her hot-headed brother Laertes, and his own talented self. In this way we must recognize the fact that there is something wrong with everyone and everything.

DON GIOVANNI, OR PROMISCUITY
RESEMBLES GRAPES

Don Giovanni, the much-publicized Spanish sportsman, playboy, man about town, loose liver, and singer has been dealt with extensively and comprehensively by such experts as Mozart, Da Ponte, Balzac, George Byron, George Bernard Shaw, and other deep thinkers.

So it would just be gilding the lily, carrying coals to Newcastle, and really redundant to rehearse the whole business of his life and works once more, except that in some respects these profound commentators seem to have missed the point. Perhaps this was because they did not have the benefit of the Kinsey Report's confusions. Most of these authors seem to be under the impression, for example, that Giovanni is having himself a wonderful time until the very end when he gets pulled down to hell screaming at the top of his voice. Before that, practically everything was fun, fun, fun.

But this is quite untrue.

He was unhappy from the very start and at the peak of his career, too. I am not speaking of the difficulty of some of his affairs of the heart, or the chancy risks he ran. The real point is that promiscuity is undiscriminating as well as indiscriminate, and Giovanni kept running against the stone wall of this fact.

Take, for example, some of his conversations with his aide-de-camp, Leporello, to whom he was wont to brag about his conquests, naturally. There was the time that he met a very beautiful girl named Alice, and in about two hours she came running across the room to him, saying: "I am going to love the pants off you!" Naturally he was delighted with Alice at the moment, and when he went home he told Leporello about her highly charged remark, and about how Alice kept a chocolate bar next to her bed at night in case she woke up because she wanted every moment to be jammed with sweetness. Naturally this made Leporello's mouth water, and he hoped that Giovanni would settle down for a while, for Alice seemed to require a good deal of attention and energy. Nothing of the kind. And Leporello should have known better. Alice told Giovanni he had to marry her or beat it, and he became very angry and told her that she was not that important to him, so that was the end of that.

Another interesting time was when Giovanni and Leporello discussed rape with a girl named Florence, who was a friend of theirs. Giovanni maintained that there was no such thing as rape, short of violence, and he inquired as to why a girl who was attacked did not kick the rude, impetuous, and unfortunate amorist in the testicles, which would certainly give him pause. "Oh, no nice girl would do that," said Florence shyly. The fact that Giovanni did not appreciate the nobility of this reply shows how little he understood women. And as Phyllis, a friend of both Giovanni and Florence, once said pensively to Florence: "All men are bastards. But some bastards are nice." Here again I think it is clear that Giovanni did not grasp the true uniqueness and profound insight of some of the girls he knew. And the reason for this blindness is that promiscuity is like the dark in that it makes all cats look gray.

The best example of how Giovanni was mixed up about what he wanted is his affair with a girl named Marlene, who was really something, partly because she seemed to be very quiet, refined, and studious. Giovanni as usual had to talk it all over with Leporello, and he told Leporello that Marlene was breaking all records. He was referring to a broad joke of which the two were very fond, and which sometimes is formulated as follows: A Frenchman says there are seventy-seven ways to make love and an amazed American says that there is just one way in America. "Comment?" asks the Frenchman. "Well, er," stammers the bashful American, "the gentleman gets on top of the lady." "Soixante-dix-huit," says the delighted Frenchman.

Well, after meeting Marlene, Giovanni kept telling Leporello how wonderful she was, and first he said sixty-nine, and then seventy-nine, and then eighty-four, ninety-six, and then one hundred and twenty-two, one hundred and forty, six hundred and fifty-one, and finally he announced that he had lost count, which of course left poor Leporello gasping like an exhausted marathon runner.

Leporello thought that anyway this time curiosity and a desire to break the world's record might keep Giovanni fixed on Marlene for a while. He was wrong again. Marlene and Giovanni had a big fight and the supposed reason was that Marlene said that Giovanni was neither flirtatious nor affectionate enough. Giovanni replied heatedly that there was a time for everything, and just as no one would expect an adult man to wear diapers, so no real lady would expect flirtation and affection every time there was any question of making love, and long after a basic understanding had been achieved. So Marlene threw him out of the house, and the irritated Giovanni told Leporello he was glad because he was getting bored with the same torso all the time.

Now the question has often been raised as to why Giovanni was like that, why he was so full of unrest, never really satisfied, always eager to make love to more and more girls, and particularly to other men's wives?

Various hypotheses have been suggested, and smirked about. It is believed by some of the latest students of the subject that Giovanni really wanted to make love to his mother and no girl ever satisfied him because of course no girl was his mother. A subtle refinement of this interpretation explains that the reason he had to go after other fellows' girls and wives is that during infancy and childhood his father was always taking his mother away from him and locking the door, so this incessant and excessive adultery was, in fact, a long revenge upon his father, and the entire male sex because his mother had preferred husband to son. Then again it is said that Giovanni found every girl to be just like his mother once he knew her, though he always hoped to find one who would be unlike his mother, so he had to run away from all of them because incest is wrong. And also there is the implausible idea that Giovanni did not like girls at all, that's why he was never satisfied with any one of them, and though this theory may seem far-fetched because of the inordinate attention Giovanni paid to the girls, lots of truths are far-fetched, like the discovery of America, for instance.

It is certainly true that Giovanni enjoyed and was much more excited by the process of courting and seducing a girl than he was excited by any actual physical reality and gratification. And it is true too that each conquest made his ego feel better, and this would also explain why he liked other men's girls. And he was undoubtedly a hit-and-run driver; once he made the girl, he was likely to beat it. All of these theories may or may not be true, but after one has reviewed all of them and weighed them critically, there is only one conclusion one can feel any certainty about, namely, that Giovanni was a Lesbian, that is to say, someone who likes to sleep with girls.

IAGO, OR THE LOWDOWN ON LIFE

Othello was a very gifted Moorish soldier who had been hired by the Venetian government to command its troops against any foreign powers that had a desire to interfere with the very profitable overseas trade of Venice. Same as ever, things don't really change.

Othello was regarded by the lords of Venice as a military genius and it was also felt by all that he was a very brave man. It was natural that the Venetian nobility should invite him to dinner and enjoy hearing stories of his experiences overseas and in strange parts of the world. Senator Brabantio invited General Othello to dinner so often that his beautiful daughter Desdemona (beautiful in character as well as from a physical standpoint) fell in love with the successful soldier.

Now in spite of all his military victories and other gratifying things in his life, Othello felt that there was something about him which made him not quite as good as the Venetian nobility. He was dark-skinned and they were on the pale side, though somewhat olive-skinned; but also it was a matter of

The Ego Is Always at the Wheel

Othello's not being well-bred or at ease in social situations the way that a Venetian gentleman would be. Given this feeling about himself, Othello was unable to perceive that Desdemona had fallen in love with him. He thought she was just interested in military strategy when she listened to the stories of his adventures, with the passion and absorption of one of those Brooklyn Dodger fans, watching the Dodgers in a crucial series against the St. Louis Cardinals.

Desdemona certainly did like Othello's stories and she admired his courage and masculinity, and perhaps she fell in love with him also because he was very strong and did not resemble her father in the least. Anyway, she was infatuated with him, and he did not have the least inkling of her feelings, and in the end Desdemona had to resort to what was a pretty cute trick, she had to tell Othello that if he had a friend who was just like him in every respect, would he please bring him to call because she would probably fall in love with him!

Othello finally took this hint which was as much of a hint as a five-o'clock steam whistle. He was overjoyed. He knew very well that the Senator would not like the prospect of such a marriage, and this may have intensified his feelings, but the couple decided to elope and they did, and everyone else, including a former suitor of Desdemona named Rollo, rejected but still quite hopeful, was very upset.

It goes without saying, human nature being what it fears, if deprived of love's fulfillment, that there was a great deal of excitement. Rollo was working hand in hand with a son of a bitch named Iago who was one of Othello's officers and did not like his superior. The two of them, Iago and Rollo, woke up the Senator in the middle of the night, right after they heard about the elopement, and in no time at all, the Senator was calling up his friends and asking that the marriage be annulled.

The clever Iago, who knew very well how to hurt people's feelings, yelled up anonymously at the Senator's window this lascivious outcry:

"A black man (ram) is tupping (on top of and having sexual intercourse with) your pure white ewe (daughter, mother, sister, virgin, and wife) (and you)," he cried at the top of his voice.

This had the expected effect on the father, and he convened the entire Venetian government at about three o'clock in the morning and demanded that they put Othello in the clink. He said that Othello must have used drugs because no well-bred Venetian girl in her right mind would marry a foreigner like that. Desdemona and Othello were summoned from the nuptial bed of their wedding night and they explained what had happened clearly and calmly, though Othello did get a little excited. The Venetian nobility were pretty much convinced, particularly by Desdemona's girlish and touching and very authentic-seeming account of what had occurred, and they thought that in any case there was no use in crying over spilt milk, what was done was done, they might as well make the best of things, especially since, as is normal, war was imminent, and Othello was a very valuable man, and they had to think of the good of the community and their investments.

The Senator was not appeased, however, and he refused to get adjusted to the inevitable like a sensible man, for his primal feelings were involved; it was as if someone had insulted his mother's honor, he had been punched in the nose of his psyche, he felt that nothing could console him, and he made one parting remark which stayed in Othello's mind and injured it the way ground glass will injure the stomach. He said to Othello that the girl had betrayed her father and would betray him, too, for a girl's attitude toward her father was the basis of the emotional pattern and behavior she brought to her husband. This shows what a handy weapon a little inexpensive and trite and false psychologizing can be.

We come now to Iago, who was really nasty, for he saw in this marriage a chance to do a great deal of harm. He disliked Othello very much, but it is not clear just why he did. He *thought* he had good reasons for disliking him and it may have seemed that he did not have good reasons, but I don't think this prevalent impression is true, because Iago was always trying to find reasons for hating and harming Othello and he was jumping from one reason to another in an effort to convince himself. The first reason was that Othello had appointed another fellow, Cassio, to be his second in command in the army, instead of giving this position to Iago who was, it can be said with reasonable certainty, superior to Cassio in knowledge and experience. But that kind of thing is always happening. And this reason for hating Othello was not very convincing really, although Iago communicated it to his friend Rollo right after Desdemona's marriage, when Rollo was in a rage and attacked Iago for permitting it to happen, as if he could have done anything about it. But Rollo was a dreadful dumb-bell, whom Iago himself had described as just poor white trash.

Now this first reason disappeared when Iago managed to get the pleasure-loving Cassio very drunk, as a result of which he was dismissed by Othello and replaced by Iago. It might be thought that this is just a superficial view for if Iago's feelings had once been very hurt, he might have remained full of hatred for Othello, even if he was afterward given what he wanted in the first place. But the fact is that Othello and Iago had become very close friends and Othello hardly did anything but praise Iago and speak warmly to him and call him honest, honest Iago, a wonderful guy.

Iago had a third reason too, for he was, as has been pointed out, desperately in quest of reasons which would justify the hatred he felt toward Othello. This third reason was his suspicion that Othello had made love successfully to Iago's wife Emilia. But it is not a very good reason either, it did not convince Iago in the least, and it is perfectly clear that he was not behaving like a jealous husband; for example, compare his behavior with the way in which Othello responded to the idea that Desdemona might have been unfaithful to him. Moreover, Iago did not act as if he cared very much about Emilia, he showed no signs whatever of affection, and one might even go so far as to say that he did not particularly like girls, he was too preoccupied with making the worst of his talent for evil and the destruction of human relationships. In fact, he was a virtuoso of evil and used his knowledge of the human heart the way a great violinist uses a Stradivarius. He certainly did like money very much and this too was so strong a preoccupation that it also suggests that he was the kind of person who does not love anyone, not even himself.

Iago was looking for reasons for justifying his hatred of Othello because he was making all sorts of subtle imputations about Desdemona, telling Othello that he did not know what to make of it but Cassio had certainly been behaving in a very friendly way toward Desdemona. The details are not important. Othello was finally convinced that his wife had slept with Cassio; he accused her, gave her no serious chance to acquit herself, choked her to death, and it all ended with Iago's treacherous destructiveness discovered, Othello brought to his senses, and committing suicide. Iago was punished, but what good did that do Othello or Desdemona?

The important thing is that Iago had no good reason for hating Othello the way he did. This is what one finds truly horrifying, though I know well enough that it goes on all the time. Iago was just evil the way that dogs bark, the sun shines, burrs stick, cats meow, and lightning strikes. Consequently poor Desdemona was dead in early youth, and for no good reason.

Now there has been some argument about whether Iago did have a good reason for hating Othello, a good reason in the sense that Othello would have had a good reason for hating Cassio, if Cassio had made love to Desdemona with her great enthusiasm, applause, and cooperation. That's what one might call a good reason. A studious fellow named Kittredge thinks that Iago did have several good reasons and takes Iago's own declarations and avowals at what is practically their face value, which was the way Othello made such a fool of himself. On the other hand, S.T. Coleridge, an expert on German philosophy, indecision, and laudanum, speaks of one of Iago's soliloquies as "the motive-hunting of a motiveless malignity." And the latter is proven right, I think, if we examine the background. Shakespeare, the brilliant country boy who wrote the Broadway hit on which this adaptation has been based, took the story from an Italian best-seller called the *Ecatommiti* by a fellow named Giovanni Battista Giraldi. Now in this short novel, which is not very good, Iago has a perfectly good reason for hating Othello: *He is a rejected suitor.* As I see it, this is conclusive: Shakespeare took the story by Giraldi and changed it when it suited his purpose. He had a perfectly good motive at hand for Iago and he omitted it, replacing it with half-hearted efforts to find motives.

Shakespeare must have known a thing or two about motives because he seems to think that the worst thing of all is not to have motives. That's what was wrong with Iago, and that is what is meant when it is said that he was really a villain, a being who does evil for its own sake.

I wonder what happened to Shakespeare or his friends, or both, to make him think of these things. Perhaps he disliked his own suspicious nature, or perhaps he did not like a world in which the innocent are unjustly choked to death, like Desdemona. He must have been a very unhappy man, even though very talented.

He seems to be saying that all he can say is that Desdemona is in her grave.

PAPERBACKS AND
THE ELIZABETHAN PARALLEL

Anyone foolish enough to remark in some literary circles that the phenomenal success of paperbacks might create a set of conditions which were virtually Elizabethan would be regarded as facetious or drunk. This is probably as it should be. To speak of a renaissance before it has occurred is more or less like discussing the future of an unborn child or the year 2054.

Yet the Elizabethan possibility is not entirely senseless, particularly if we think in terms of a set of conditions rather than of great authors. The success of paperbacks is bound to remind anyone who has taught modern literature to undergraduates during the past generation, that students often possess a greater passion for literature than the rest of the population, a passion ordinarily reserved for the major league pennant races. The truth is that most students can be quickly persuaded to read any novel or poem, however difficult, obscure, intellectual, or highbrow. Indeed, the problem sometimes becomes one of persuading the student that good books were written before 1900, and that a poem is not necessarily good because it is obscure, or bad because it is simple.

What happens to these students when they are through with school? The answer, in part, is that the act of reading is a solitary one. In a physical sense, at least, it separates one from other human beings; and if one reads the kind of book which others do not, the separation is more than physical. As long as the student is in school, he can talk about the books he reads in class and to other students. Once he is done with school, there is the risk that he will be talking about something which others know nothing about. The activities which one can talk about are manifold, and gradually or swiftly they tend to supplant an activity about which, at best, one cannot talk freely.

The important point about paperbacks is the evidence that many more human beings like to read than was commonly assumed, an assumption reinforced long ago by *Middletown*, the sociological study by the Lynds of a typical Midwestern community. In Middletown, the belief prevailed that anyone who read a great deal was extremely peculiar and probably addicted to secret vices.

It may seem unreasonable, but when hundreds of thousands of human beings do the same thing, it ceases to be peculiar. Some of the reasons for the paperback revolution are fairly clear, and not purely economic, since the public library provides books for nothing. The purchase of a paperback is a casual act, involving no pretensions and no great emotional stake. The paperback reader's only desire is pleasure, and he is not likely to be suspected of being an intellectual or a highbrow, as he might be if he frequented the public library. He feels no solemn duty toward the paperback and he does not feel that his intelligence is at fault if it bores him, since it has not been presented as a monument of human culture which confers superiority upon the reader.

It is true enough that a great many paperbacks are trash. But a good many are not. It is also true that most paperback readers do not discriminate between William Faulkner and James M. Cain. But the lack of discrimination cuts both ways. The reader may not know the difference between Faulkner and Cain, but he reads both. Being perforce a literary critic, I cannot regard this as the perfect state of affairs. But at the same time, I cannot believe that undiscriminating reading is not more desirable than no reading at all. In a like way, the idea that one ought to read only masterpieces represents a very narrow, one-sided conception of literature.

It will be said, of course, that paperbacks are popular because they are full of sex and violence: But this is precisely what the Elizabethan playwright depended upon and what I mean by the Elizabethan parallel. As long as the reader's interest is awakened and sustained, he will read anything.

"In a play of Shakespeare," T.S. Eliot said (and we need only substitute: in a novel by Faulkner), "you get several levels of significance. For the simplest auditor there is the plot; for the more thoughtful the character and the conflict of character; for the more musically sensitive the rhythm; for the more literary the words and the phrasing; and for the auditors of greater sensitiveness and understanding, a meaning which gradually reveals itself . . . the sensitiveness of every auditor is acted upon by all these elements, but in different degrees of consciousness."

This is merely the description of a possibility. There are many difficulties now which did not exist in 1590. But paperbacks lessen these difficulties in ways which Broadway, Hollywood, the radio, and television do not, since reading a book requires a different kind of attention. There is no reason, certainly, for wild optimism, but it is equally unquestionable that a new cultural situation is emerging. It is possible that the bad books will drive out the good books. It is also possible that the curiosity of the lowbrow will sustain the passion of the student as it supports the serious writer.

THE NAMING OF A HOTEL

This is a true story. It is also a very prudent one, the kind that is sometimes termed, I believe, "a cautionary tale," for it shows, among other things, how dangerous it is to be an editor and a literary critic. It also shows how dangerous it is *not* to be an editor and a literary critic.

In 1945, when I was one of the three editors of *Partisan Review*, a friend of mine brought me the typescript of a story by a young writer who was later to become famous and to express, when he became famous, an unqualified detestation of all literary critics. My friend asked me to read the story, consider it as submitted to *Partisan Review*, and, if I found it unworthy of the extremely high standards of the magazine, to write a note to the young writer, making clear my reasons for rejecting it.

I read the story, found it quite unbearable, and wrote a brief note explaining that it seemed "unrealistic" to me, since at one point the protagonist drinks martinis and then eats oysters and then the oysters turn to stone in his stomach.

The Ego Is Always at the Wheel

The young writer sent me, soon after, a five-page letter of denunciation, which is still in my possession and which I contemplate from time to time, although it is neither well-written nor just.

I answered the letter with a calm and objectivity I did not feel, pointing out that it was impossible for an editor to write detailed critiques of very many of the manuscripts submitted to him, for if he did, he would not be able to perform other editorial tasks or do any work of his own. It was true, I added, that my own work was regarded as worthless by at least one other writer, but this was a judgment which I could not accept, at least for the time being.

Several years passed. During those years, both I and the young writer toiled, unlike the lilies of the field, in the vineyards of literature. But he waxed and I waned. He flourished exceedingly when his first novel, *End As a Man*, appeared and became a national best-seller, and Mr. Calder Willingham (for it was he) became a famous young American novelist.

Several more years passed. Willingham continued to flourish and I continued to be an editor and literary critic. An important personal change did, however, occur: I became addicted to the reading of paperbacks, partly, I think, as a refuge from the occupational hazard of reading highbrow typescripts by young and unbearably arrogant young writers. I soon found that I delighted in paperbacks of all kinds, but that I preferred Gold Medal Books—which are, I think, supposed by most readers to be the worst kind of paperbacks—to any other kind. They very often seemed the best of all possible paperbacks to me, but perhaps this was partly because I was engaged in unconscious flight from egghead fiction, literary criticism, and the *avant-garde*.

Be this as it may, one day I purchased the first paperback

edition of *End As a Man*. I supposed I was moved by morbid curiosity as to the merits of one of my severist critics. Perhaps he was right and I was wrong: He was certainly right if the chief criterion was prosperity, literary and economic. And then, long before I had a chance to decide on whether or not I had been wrong about Mr. Willingham's narrative genius—in a purely objective, and yet also purely private and unofficial way—I came upon a description of a house of ill-fame frequented by the young gentlemen who are the leading characters of *End As a Man*. The house of ill-fame was named the Hotel Delmore! I read no more in that book that day, nor have I ever after been able to read Mr. Willingham's other works of fiction. It was hard to believe then, and it has continued to be hard to believe, that anyone was capable of so much outrageous innocence.

Soon after, however, I did speak of the name of the hotel to a young writer who was a close friend of Willingham's. I said that the naming of the hotel had doubtless been the unconscious expression of personal resentment, but it was certainly extreme personal resentment and entirely unjustified, since I had never run a hotel of any kind.

Mr. Willingham, upon being told of my comment, replied with characteristic indignation that the naming of the hotel was not in the least unconscious; he had deliberately chosen the name while wholly conscious of what he was doing. He felt that he had every right as an author to vent his anger at me personally for having rejected him, although he would not have done so if the name of the hotel was not exactly right from an artistic point of view.

SURVEY OF OUR
NATIONAL PHENOMENA

The public's intense interest in a person, a pastime, or an idea is one of the most familiar and important occurrences in American life. For weeks, for months, sometimes for years, one person or thing is a topic of conversation, a seed-bed of jokes, an object of passionate curiosity or of some other emotion that preoccupies the public mind. When this happens, we have what can only be called a national phenomenon.

At the moment, Grace Kelly and Marilyn Monroe have returned to the limelight of public attention. Each of these screen stars has been a national phenomenon for some time, but other national phenomena took public attention until the announcement of Miss Kelly's engagement to the Prince of Monaco and the news that Miss Monroe would co-star with Sir Laurence Olivier.

It is characteristic that both stars have moved in an international direction. This is often true of American national phenomena, and often enough they come from abroad. A few short months ago the Princess Margaret's romance was in the foreground of public attention.

Over the years the origin of a national phenomenon has been of every variety and kind, native and foreign. Sometimes it is crossword puzzles or a new game such as Scrabble; sometimes a new crooner, a new cartoon, a new gangster, or a new kind of eccentric. Any complete list for the past thirty years would have to include baby sitters, flag-pole sitters, child stars, boy wonders, quiz kids, channel swimmers, and the kings and queens of Europe, as well as great scientists and thinkers.

It is actually more often a person than a thing which engrosses the public sufficiently to achieve the status of a national phenomenon. And the attempt to explain why one person, rather than another one with many of the same traits, attracts the public leads to speculations which are interesting even when they can hardly be regarded as conclusive. If the attempt to explain a national phenomenon is a guessing game more often than not, it can be, like most games, illuminating and valuable, whether one is right or wrong.

Marilyn Monroe is a good example of the difficulty in explaining why a personality becomes a national phenomenon. None of the customary reasons for an actress' success and fame can explain very much when applied to Miss Monroe.

She is a very pretty girl, of course, but there are a great many pretty girls who cannot, no matter how hard they try, attract the same kind of attention. She has a very winning personality, but this explains very little compared with the impact of Tallulah Bankhead and Martha Raye. She is often a good actress, better by far than she is usually credited with being, but this does not account for her success as it does for the triumphs of Audrey Hepburn and Julie Harris. The most obvious explanation—the open display of sexual attractiveness—is also unconvincing in itself. Miss Monroe does not exactly conceal her person, but Gypsy Rose Lee and Sally Rand, among others, have outstripped (no other word is exact) Miss Monroe by far, and Mae West and Gwen Verdon have dramatized sexual awareness with a knowledge and explicitness entirely beyond Miss Monroe.

As one young starlet asked, with annoyance and pretension, "What has Marilyn got? And how can I get it?"

A large part of the answer lies in Miss Monroe's attitude toward herself. Along with her very evident feminine charms goes a genuine delight in being sexually attractive—an attitude that makes attractiveness seem as natural as sunlight. No amount of connections and calculated exploitation of beauty could achieve the same effect.

Miss Kelly is a symbol in a very different way. The heroines she plays take the sexual initiative in a remarkably overt way, but always as perfectly proper young ladies. It is as if a not-nice girl, when in love, would behave otherwise and no well-bred wife would act otherwise toward her husband. Female interest in physical love becomes respectable and proper, as if no one had ever thought it vulgar and immodest in a good woman. The nice girl as coquette or flirt is archaic and coy.

No one can get to be a national phenomenon by mere effort, love, or money. Ambition, talent, the best of intentions, or the most sensational of crimes do not suffice very often. They may make a human being a newspaper sensation for a few weeks or win the attention of posterity, but they cannot establish anyone in that special relationship to the public which is a necessary characteristic of a national phenomenon.

The Ego Is Always at the Wheel

The failure of the effort to make Marion Davies a favorite film star with the public is a good example of how the status of a national phenomenon is often beyond the most lavish expenditures for publicity and film production. A contrary instance, the transformation of John D. Rockefeller, Sr. from a "robber baron" to a leading philanthropist was managed, it is true, by a conscious plan, but it occurred after the active financial career, and it is possible that the dime tips he gave ultimately tickled the public's fancy with an effectiveness which exceeded that of the philanthropic gifts of $446,719,571.22.

A national phenomenon is sometimes a person of genuine genius or eminence; he is often, however, a mediocrity and sometimes the status is thrust upon him for freakish, bizarre, eccentric, questionable, or lawless behavior, as in the instances of Jesse James, Annie Oakley, Carry Nation, Al Capone, and Frank Costello.

This is one important reason for use of "national phenomenon" as a phrase: It has an independent meaning even though it sometimes refers to someone who is also a hero or a star, a great inventor, a great author, or a notorious criminal. Some of the most gifted human beings do not achieve the status during their lives, while their less gifted contemporaries do. Horatio Alger's novels gave him a national eminence of a sort, but Henry James—although he yearned for the kind of popularity Dickens enjoyed—was disappointed all his life by the failure of his novels.

The late Frederick Lewis Allen provides a number of illustrations of what a national phenomenon is in *Only Yesterday*, his social history of the Nineteen Twenties, a period in which—perhaps because the public was being made more aware of the American scene than ever before—national phenomena appeared in abundance.

Lindbergh is perhaps Mr. Allen's most clear-cut example. Mr. Allen does not in the least underestimate Lindbergh's courage and heroism in flying the Atlantic, but he is also impressed by the fanatical public enthusiasm for the flier, which differed so from the attention attracted by those who performed the same feat soon afterward. Only Lindbergh excited such remarks as the *New York Evening World's* assertion that his flight was "the greatest feat of a solitary man in the history of the human race." For years to come, one could criticize Coolidge, Hoover, Ford, Bobby Jones, and other headliners, but an unfavorable remark about Lindbergh was regarded as blasphemous or obscene.

Mr. Allen's convincing explanation is that for years the public had been spiritually starved, deprived of its hopes and ideals. The past had been debunked and the present was continually revealed as sordid or scandalous. Thus, although Mr. Allen does not call Lindbergh a national phenomenon or refer directly to the American Dream, his explanation clearly relates the one to the other as the reason that Lindbergh became an idol overnight. His flight was a swift, indisputable demonstration that the American Dream was still alive, that the courage, initiative, and self-reliance of the solitary individual might still accomplish new wonders.

Yet this example of the rise from obscurity to the limelight, from rags to riches, does not represent the only manifestation of the American Dream. There can be less pleasant but equally typical experiences arising from a given American mood.

The remark attributed to Barnum, "There's a sucker born every minute," and Texas Guinan's greeting to her night-club patrons, "Hello, suckers," indicate that although hope and optimism are the attitudes most attractive to the public, an ironic and hard-boiled attitude toward too much hope and optimism has a characteristic and recurrent appeal also. And in times of extreme crisis, when depression or war seem an unending threat or a termination of the American Dream's premise of life, liberty, and happiness, such figures as Huey Long and Gerald L. K. Smith come to the fore.

This kind of rationale must not, however, be pursued too far too lightly. As the pollsters discovered in 1948, it is easy to be wrong about the mood of a nation which includes, among its manifold differences, the difference between a native of Maine and a native of Texas. A national mood (on large affairs) and a national phenomenon (in popular interest) may coincide in time, but it is not always possible to relate the one to the other in terms of causation.

With these qualifications in mind, it may be interesting to look further into some of the personalities who now or in the recent past can be called national phenomena. The choices have been made partly to show that the phrase has an independent meaning, although it has not hitherto been formally defined. They have also been made because the examples in question are related to one another as significant of the public's changing attitudes.

To call Willie Mays a national phenomenon, but to say Jackie Robinson is not, is to risk rocking Ebbets Field and enraging all of Brooklyn. Yet the comparison helps show the difference between a baseball player who is a national phenomenon and one who is simply a great star. (Actually, if skill were the only criterion, the first choice would have to be Ted Williams; he is probably the greatest batter since Babe Ruth.)

Robinson was chosen as the first Negro major leaguer because of his courage as well as his ability. Both qualities are evident in his style of play; his daring base-running, his delight in rattling the pitcher and umpire are part of an entirely justified aggressiveness, for which ball players are praised. But Robinson, in his pioneering role, was very much a symbol of an oppressed minority, a symbol akin—though in a lesser degree—to that presented by the great Negro boxers.

Willie Mays' personality and his accomplishments are in direct contrast. When his cap falls off while he is running the bases, or when he makes the kind of spectacular catch and throw which inspired a sportswriter to say in 1961, "It must be a wonderful thing to be twenty years old and have the reflexes of a mountain lion!", he appears to the public purely as an enchanting and remarkable human being.

This explanation has the virtue, at least, of making it seem not incongruous to speak next of President Eisenhower as a national phenomenon. He possessed this status, as many Presidents and military leaders—however eminent—have not, long before his election, because of a personal quality which shows itself as that of a human being who not only does not act or talk like a general, but does not act or talk like a politician.

It is the same attractiveness which is responsible for the fact that, although the dignity of office makes the public speak of President Eisenhower, it has always thought of him as Ike, never as Dwight.

Adlai Stevenson's emergence as a national phenomenon in 1952 can be summarized in one word: Egghead. Whether or not it was suggested by the oval shape of his bald head, the significant thing was the necessity for a new word, instead of intellectual, longhair, or highbrow. Since the college-educated population has more than doubled in forty years, and since so many intellectuals now have crew cuts, "longhair" has lost even its visual meaning; receding hairlines, meanwhile, have taken away any possible imputations to "highbrow."

Some of Mr. Stevenson's predecessors in national politics were intellectuals. Theodore Roosevelt certainly was one and took pride in being one, but he dramatized himself so successfully as he-man-of-the-great-outdoors that when he became President, Mark Hanna said of this patrician Harvard man and disciple of Henry Adams, "Now that damn cowboy is in the White House."

Mr. Stevenson's candid unselfconsciousness as an intellectual is very different from Woodrow Wilson's eloquence. Wilson spoke with a solemnity becoming in a professor who resembled not only a stern schoolmaster but a clergyman. Mr. Stevenson's genuine informality and his fondness for a wisecrack are typical of the new breed of intellectuals. Professors are now preoccupied rather than absent-minded, intellectuals are no longer impractical cranks and crackpots. The new public attitude becomes clear if you ask this leading question: "Which would you rather be, an egghead or a blockhead?"

Similarly, authorship not only has become free of the stigma of eccentricity in recent years, but is now one of the most glamorous of professions. Ernest Hemingway's career, for example, is the complete embodiment of all that makes a writer seem a privileged being. He is a national phenomenon as few Americans have been and as other equally important authors are not. Hemingway is one of his own heroes to the public; he not only talks and acts like them but, as one who has almost been killed more often than any other well-known person, even surpasses them.

In another field, though still somewhat bookish, there have been, recurrently, the Kinsey studies of sexual behavior.

These might conceivably have been made in another era, but it is hard to believe that they would have been available to the public, and openly discussed previous to the social changes and revised attitudes which have made divorce, for example, seem at times a painful necessity rather than a social stigma.

The personal quality that makes Professor Kinsey a national phenomenon appears in his books, but is far more evident when he expounds his aims in a conducted tour of his laboratory at Indiana University. He speaks of the most intimate matters, long regarded in silence or embarrassment, with the matter-of-factness and openness of Elmer Davis reporting political events. The tone, like Mr. Davis', is that of an old-fashioned liberal, and the motives of compassion and sympathy are as unquestionable as the chief social aim of his work to provide a scientific basis for a greater degree of tolerance—an aim which is as characteristically American as our faith in facts and figures and the belief that statistics don't lie.

There is certainly no direct connection between Professor Kinsey and such stars as Marilyn Monroe and Grace Kelly, except that they have won the intense attention of the same public. Since that public was impressed rather than scandalized by Professor Kinsey's absolute sincerity and realistic honesty, it may be for related reasons that the public made Miss Monroe and Miss Kelly famous overnight.

When any new national phenomenon appears, demonstrating again that lightning may strike anyone from Shirley Temple to Grandma Moses, or when an attempt to fabricate one fails (proving that you can't fool most of the people most of the time), it is natural to remember *e pluribus unum* and the American Dream as well.

It is perhaps not possible to draw any firm lessons from all this. But there are certain clues that are worth considering.

The Ego Is Always at the Wheel

For one thing, the mere existence of a national phenomenon indicates a degree of national homogeneity; despite our vast geography, we can all share an intense interest in a person or thing, although our individual reactions to it may vary.

Second, a national phenomenon is often the most spontaneous manifestation of the democratic process, because it is an expression of the public's moods and aspirations, hopes and fears. Would this not be a fruitful field for inquiry—an attempt to equate a given interest with its contemporary setting? Are our interests the same in times of economic well-being as they are in times of economic hardship? Certainly there were well-defined "crazes" or fads that sprang up during the depression of the Nineteen Thirties. What is the connection between bread and circuses?

Finally, national phenomena are important, perhaps most of all, as a means of communication and knowledge. Each of us is part of the public in one or another way, but it is the emergence of a new national phenomenon which makes the individual aware of the entire public, helps him to know he is part of that public, and shows him what he has in common with others and how he differs from them.

Unless we know what preoccupies other human beings and excites their concern and admiration, we can hardly be said to know them: And it is an old truth that when one does not know others, one hardly has any knowledge of oneself. Millions of Americans, otherwise separate from or unknown to one another, communicate their most intimate feelings when the voice of the people is heard in the land, discussing the latest national phenomena, the newly-risen stars of American life.

STREETCAR, THE METAPHOR

It seems that for many years, and perhaps during every year that I have known, and perhaps for years without number and henceforth, I have been doing the same doing and will be performing the same activity, again and again. It is thus very reasonable for me to think that on the first day that I did this thing, that day, that very day, was my birthday, and not the December day written on my birth-certificate and much discussed in our family. For then, at that time, when I began to breathe, have pain and appetite, and cry, then was hardly the proper beginning, if in fact there is such a thing as a beginning and an end (for he who is actually beginning, if he is beginning, does not know that he is beginning, and who will be daring and presumptuous enough to discuss with certainty that which is called the ending?—I mean to say that we never have the experience of a beginning or an ending: We merely speak of it).

Once, when younger than now, I read long in a great library the newspapers of my birthday to find out what else had happened upon that day. But this is another story.

When I was three years of age, we lived in a Brooklyn apartment, and the living room was at right angles to an avenue on which a streetcar shook its jangling voyage. Placed often on the window-sill to be amused by the street (for how long, now, the streets do not amuse me), I was particularly enchanted by this yellow and red object, schooner, or caterpillar, moving one way and moving back again. It was very beautiful to me, it seems. The proof is that one day a friend of my mother's, a lady named Mrs. Salmon, who had given me a spoon (a spoon, mind you) on my first birthday, came to visit us, proudly with her son's fiancée, her beautiful daughter-in-law to be. I looked long at the young lady who was very pretty in a cold and black-haired way and very shy (perhaps I am shy for this reason), and then, delighted by the plump young baby (who filled her with such pleasant thoughts of futurity, perhaps), she kissed him, and he said out loud, with a lisp and yet with unheard thunder, announcing the whole activity and devotion of his life: "STREETCAR!"

MEMOIRS OF A METROPOLITAN CHILD, MEMOIRS OF A GIANT FAN

A long time has passed since I lived through the throes of childhood and early adolescence on Washington Heights, near Coogan's Bluff and thus near the Polo Grounds. Literally or chronologically, the years from 1921 to 1928 are either a long time or a short time, depending upon how one feels about oneself; whether one is happy now or suffered from an unhappy childhood then. But it is a very long time in a way which has nothing to do with personal experience. I myself sometimes feel as if the years of boyhood had occurred early in the nineteenth century, and I feel, as the poet said, that I have more memories than if I had lived for a thousand years. This is personal, however, although others may feel precisely as I do. The era of great prosperity was naturally enough a time of overwhelming optimism; now, in 1958, it is difficult to believe that many human beings do not know that they are living through the most apocalyptic and terrifying century since the fall of Rome.

When I was a boy, it seemed entirely obvious to me that

everything was getting better and better in every way, day by day, especially if one lived in Manhattan and was a Giant fan. Hence, I was neither impressed nor astonished to read in the newspaper that a French doctor and psychologist named Dr. Coué had arrived in the New World and suggested immediately that everyone adopt an attitude of supreme and unqualified optimism towards all problems and every kind of difficulty or pain. He said—or I think I remember that he said—that one had only to say to oneself that everything was getting better every day in every way, then what one wanted to happen was precisely what would happen: The dogma of optimism would make the pursuit of happiness a great actuality which continually and increasingly surpassed itself.

Dr. Coué's optimism impressed partly because he did not live on Washington Heights and root for the Giants. I felt pity and compassion for the human beings of Brooklyn, Philadelphia, St. Louis, San Francisco, Europe, Asia, and Africa and all the unfortunate generations of mankind who had been born before the twentieth century. My natural juvenile optimism comprehended all things, as Dr. Coué advised, and it was supported by incontestable objects and events, particularly on Washington Heights. For these were the years when the George Washington Bridge and the Medical Center were being built, and for the four years 1921, 1922, 1923, and 1925, the Giants won four pennants in a row, something which had never before happened in major league baseball. Many other objects, inventions, events, and occurrences seemed to me merely instances and proofs of a conviction which I had never questioned. Everything was getting better and better all the time: Everything was getting better and richer and more exciting and more important and more heroic: The radio came into existence, Gertrude Ederle swam the English Channel, Lindbergh flew the Atlantic alone, the League of Nations labored to prevent any future war, bigotry was medieval, medicine cured more and more diseases, and these forms of continual progress seemed neither more nor less significant than electric ice boxes, elevators, the saxophone, Hollywood actresses, or the idolatrous admiration which some of the teachers in school excited in me. One of them, a young married lady, made an impression upon me which has never been quite removed, because she was a descendent of one of the signers of the Constitution, she was very pretty and she read *The New York Times* for the first hour of every morning. The public schools had already begun to be overcrowded and as a result there were more and more Rapid Advance classes. Time and again, I was promoted to a Rapid Advance class. At one point when, through indolence and a misguided unsuccessful effort to be one of the Bad Boys instead of one of the Nice Boys, I was promoted to an ordinary class, hardly more than a month of the term had passed, before the Assistant Principal arrived and conferred with the teacher and shifted five students, including myself, to a newly-formed Rapid Advance class. This occurred in 1924 and the *mystique* which governed my mind then made me think of the Giants' four consecutive pennants and of being one of the pupils who belonged to the elite of the Rapid Advance classes as manifestations of the same process of a very pleasant present reality. I ignored or dismissed the fact that the Giants had lost to the Yankees in the World Series of 1923 and 1924, just as I quickly forgot poor grades in arithmetic and sinus headaches: It was easy to forget these unpleasant occurrences as soon as they were over.

By 1926 I was a student in a *senior* high school—the difference between being a student at a senior high school and at a junior high school or just a public school pupil was immense: It had long since overpowered the imagination: It was virtually comparable to the difference between the major and the minor leagues, and between being a star and a benchwarmer or a second-string catcher. I also had come, some time before that, to the conclusion that I ought to be a poet and a dramatic critic not only when I was an adult, but as soon as possible. I intended to practice those two vocations for five months of the year, from October until March, writing poems during the day and going to all the first nights on Broadway every evening. From April until October, I intended to be the Giants' shortstop and after a time, when John J. McGraw retired, I planned to succeed him as the Giants' manager. Other important vocations tempted me, but I felt that I might not have the time to do justice to all of them.

I felt that I had already commenced to be a poet, dramatic critic, and ballplayer during the summer in camp, by writing poems in private, composing reviews of the Saturday night shows for the camp newspaper, and playing third base for the camp ball team in so authoritative and comprehensive a way that the shortstop said he had nothing to do and the baseball counsellor told me to stop acting as manager of the camp team by holding pointless conferences with the pitcher every time he looked nervous. In a like way, the counsellor who edited the camp newspaper told me that unless I stopped praising the cast of each Saturday night show in so many superlatives—and stopped praising my brother and myself most of all whenever we were in the play—he would either make me his sports reporter or get along without me entirely.

My first term at senior high school seemed as portentous and significant as the journey, in nineteenth century novels, of the hero to a city from the provincial town where he had grown to manhood in the heart of his family. Most important of all, perhaps, was the fact that one no longer ate lunch at home, one travelled by streetcar to school, and hence one's spending money had to be much greater than it had ever been before. Suddenly I had access to secret purchasing power, which I wanted very much so that I would be able to buy books and go to the Polo Grounds as a full-fledged paid admission as soon as the baseball season began.

The books that I wanted to buy were all written by H. L. Mencken; the neighborhood circulating library possessed only one of these books, *Prejudices: Second Series*. It was only years after that the complete meaning of prejudices became unpleasant and exact for me—and my passion to read the other four volumes of the series became more intense every month, on the day that the green-covered number of *The American Mercury* appeared, for each one contained a new pronouncement by Mencken which enchanted me. The enchantment was in all truth a spell, a state of fascination or of hypnotism, for when Mencken said that all poets were liars, that America was awful, that war was a benefit to mankind, I remained untroubled. It was as if he had said something else and something which was pleasing and impressive: Indeed I think that my pleasure in all of his utterances had little to do with the explicit meaning of his writings, for he said a good many statements which, if they had been written or spoken by any other human being, would have infuriated me, or seemed the formulations of a fool and a criminal. He was not only a wonderful buffoon in his writing, but unlike all the other comedians I had known or seen on the silver screen, an intellectual clown who made fun of most intellectuals and most ideas, which sufficed to make him seem all the more superior: He was superior to other writers, other comedians, and his ideas were superior to the ideas of other men: Otherwise, he would not have made fun of them in ways which became more and more irresistible.

It was H. L. Mencken's authority—his mild praise, in an advertisement which appeared in *The American Mercury* of another editor's periodical (*E. J. Haldemann's Monthly*) which made me seek for the latter periodical in the high school library, for praise from Mencken, however mild, was so rare as to seem unique. At first I was unable to find anything in any number of *E. J. Haldemann's Monthly* which seemed to justify any praise whatever, or to possess the delightful exuberance and casual superiority with which Mencken, and sometimes some of his writers, wrote. But then, as I searched carefully through number after number, convinced that what was praised by H. L. Mencken must certainly be very good writing and that it was some failing in me which kept me from recognizing what was praise amid so much hilarious scorn and contempt, I encountered an essay which summarized a book which had just been translated into English, Oswald Spengler's *The Decline of the West*. I read the summary four times, becoming more and more distressed at each reading. For Spengler, according to his exponent, had a view of the whole of history, of the twentieth century and of the future, which was not only in direct contradiction to all that I knew or believed, but which, worst of all, excluded the possibility of genuine poetry or genuine creative activity during the twentieth century or on the part of any human being who had been born during this century. The last important writer, according to Spengler, was George Bernard Shaw: Western Civilization had begun to decline, and although it would not fall until a great many years in the future, its existence would come to an end sooner or later. This had certainly happened to the great civilizations of Greece and Rome and to all other civilizations. For every civilization was mortal and its existence, like that of a human being, was subject to the same cycle of birth, growth, fruition, decline, and death; or spring, summer, autumn, and winter.

According to Spengler or his exponent, Western civilization had reached autumn; it was the time of harvest and the reaping of the benefits of Western civilization's energy during the spring and summer of our culture, while all new writers were bound to be fourth-rate imitators of the truly great. What most impressed and distressed me was the use of analogy. George Bernard Shaw was the equivalent of Aristophanes; Goethe was the Western Plato: Since I knew almost nothing about these authors and Spengler seemed to be a man of colossal learning—he knew even more than H. L. Mencken—he was probably right. Worst of all, the autumn and decline of Classical civilization had begun when most human beings lived in huge cities like Rome and were passionate about bread and circuses, instead of being farmers and participating in the Olympic games. The analogy between Roman circuses and major league baseball was incontestable and unbearable. Both were games in which the populace participated as spectators and not as players. Important was the fact that the citizens of New York and Rome were not farmers and engaged in as little physical labor as possible. This made them indolent, pleasure-loving, and incapable of producing a great poet.

After weeks of extreme anxiety about the present and the future, I began to be very attentive in the history class and I embarked upon a plan of action which, I thought, might prove that Spengler was wrong. The plan of action consisted of an elaborate schedule of rigorous and aescetic practices; one of them was walking home from school every day, and thus becoming strong and self-sufficient. Since I already had good economic and literary reasons for walking home from school, and the distance from high school to the apartment house where I lived was a mere thirty-seven blocks, this proved almost too easy and I felt that a greater austerity was necessary: I would be getting nowhere unless I also walked *to* school every morning. This would not only make me strong and self-sufficient twice as fast, but it would also double my purchasing power.

In a short time I discovered that I had gone too far. The walking to school made me late for classes and was the cause of a disastrous increase of appetite at lunch: The money saved on carfare was spent on sandwiches and chocolate bars. I succeeded in a difficult stabilization of the entire situation by getting up very early in the morning, so that I would not be late to school, and by bringing sandwiches and fruit in my briefcase. I ate the sandwiches and fruit in a state of shame at lunchtime, feeling that I was guilty of a secret and unworthy action; the action was inspired by an exalted purpose, but the other boys with whom I ate lunch supposed that I was very hungry, very poor, and quite peculiar.

Nevertheless, walking itself was a triumphant progress, and I attracted the attention of the history teacher by asking questions in class which he was astonished and pleased to be asked and to answer. He was used to being asked very few questions and reduced very often by his students' indifference or lack of preparation to asking simple questions and getting ridiculous answers. A month after the beginning of the term, he had asked a simple question based upon the assigned reading and received so many ludicrous answers that he paused, said nothing, attempted to suppress his feelings, and finally made what I took to be an extremely ironic remark to the entire class. "When you don't know the answer," he told us, "say Asia Minor. You are likely to be right more often than not." The class laughed, feeling that this was a very witty remark. That was years ago, and during the past five years this teacher's ironic advice has come to seem less and less amusing, unless a tragic truth is also a joke, and blowing up of the Suez Canal can be viewed as a practical joke, and Nassar can be dismissed as merely a clown.

The questions I asked in class were attempts to find information which would prove that Spengler was wrong; although these questions were often unrelated to the immediate subject being discussed in class, and seemed very strange to the other students, nevertheless, the curiosity and intensity with which I asked the questions were so genuine, and I seemed so interested in the answers, that the teacher was pleased, although somewhat perplexed and amazed.

My interest in the fate of Western civilization and in Spengler soon became so much of a preoccupation that I paid less and less attention to H.L. Mencken and the news of trades and other transactions of the Hot Stove league as reported in the sporting section of the newspapers. The more I walked and the more I found out about the history of civilization, the more I thought the city was unfriendly and distant, a frequent occurrence which I could hardly disregard as I crossed each street and which seemed to me to be vast and mobile and ubiquitous evidence that Spengler was right.

This obsession with history, civilization, the future, and pedestrianism began in October 1926. The year after, when Lindbergh flew the Atlantic alone—"the greatest feat of a single man in all history," according to the *New York World*—I probably would have been able to believe in the power of the individual to escape mediocrity by his own effort, no matter how other human beings behaved. But as a student of the national game and a Giant fan, I believed in stars and heroes— as did the sportswriters, to judge by their accounts of the pennant race and particularly of the World Series. Nevertheless, baseball was a team game, teamwork was very important, and even the best pitcher or batter was clearly unable to win the pennant himself. I also had been continually encouraged by reading the superlatives with which books were advertised and which never failed to hail various modern novelists and dramatists as having surpassed Dickens, Tolstoy, George Eliot, and Sophocles. This seemed as natural as the clear superiority of the automobile to the horse and buggy.

During this period of doubt and fear, however, everything which had seemed to be overwhelming proof of the superiority of the present to the past had become exactly the opposite. The progress of science and the inventions of industrialism was precisely what Spengler himself had said was proof that the dismal future belonged to engineers, scientists, and millionaires. By this time I had found a circulating library which contained a copy of the huge volume of Spengler's *The Decline of the West,* and although it was written in too abstruse a style for me to be able to read much of it—a failure which deepened my gloom—Spengler had included fascinating and fearful charts at the end of the book. These charts showed the parallels between the birth, growth, decline, and fall of past civilizations and also included Western civilization until 1920. The blanks which came after 1920 were abysses; and next to them, on each chart, were the fearful historical parallels which recorded the inevitable decline and fall of past civilizations.

By December, the cold and the rain made walking more

arduous and unpleasant, but my determination continued and grew. Before encountering Spengler, the famous men I most admired were John J. McGraw, H. L. Mencken, Thomas Alva Edison, and Sherlock Holmes, being not only untroubled by the fact that Holmes was a creature of a novelist's imagination, but supposing that Sir Arthur Conan Doyle was exactly like his own hero and lived the same dazzling, omniscient life: In fact, it seemed not in the least an accident that both McGraw and Holmes were often called master-minds. But Spengler now surpassed all of these idols and what is more, made me forget about them. The admiration I felt for Spengler differed from all previous feelings of admiration. It was admiration and detestation at the same time. I was not only in awe of him, but afraid of him, for he had pronounced the doom of the future and my own doom. Moreover, I had never before encountered an author whom I was unable to read and understand: Often enough, I had only had the illusion of being able to understand what I read. Spengler relieved me of the possibility of self-delusion because he used so many words and referred to so many things I knew nothing about; and whenever I was able to understand a sentence or a paragraph, the meaning of his text was an annihilation of hope, expectation, ambition, and the future.

It will have occurred to some readers—to those who are very much like myself—that I was going to great lengths, in more ways than one, to deal with the future, particularly with my own distant future. And it is almost needless to add that the grandiose character of my efforts to assure and reassure myself would justify the most charitable reader to remark: "What a precocious egomaniac!" I must confess that I feel the truth of this judgment is inescapable, and there would be no point in denying or defending myself. It would be senseless to say that all other human beings, particularly in adolescence, are governed by the same delusions of grandeur, because it is certainly not true of all other human beings. Most human beings live lives of quiet resignation. No apology, defense, or extenuation is possible. But an explanation, which is far from being the same as a justification, may help others to understand the fondness I feel—and the freedom from shame—when I remember my efforts to cope with Spengler, history, the future, and hope.

The quality of American life, especially as it is expressed in advertisements, which I read carefully as if each ad was composed of descriptive and exact prose, was full of colossal superlatives. And then the newspapers were full of reports of boy wonders and child prodigies, which made me feel that I was rather slow in getting started and perhaps would never get started at all. A young lady, who was just six months older than I, had published two important books of poetry, and when I read her poems, I was not only much impressed, but her work seemed so good and so accomplished that I was afraid I might be no poet at all, either then or in the future. And finally the desire to be a poet was one which I had concealed for several years, like a secret vice, as a result of the attitude of the other boys on the block or in school and above all as a result of the comment of one of my close relatives when I spoke of wanting to become a poet. "How can you become a poet?" this relative asked with utmost sincerity and good will. "Was your father a poet? Was your grandfather a poet?" And then, to console me and salve the dismay which must have been obvious upon my face, I was told that there was no point in being a poet anyway, since it was not in the least a lucrative pursuit. This consolation fell on deaf ears, since I expected to be paid very well as a regular on the

Giants. But the latter expectation suggested evading the ruthless logic of the questions which pained me. I thought of the fact that many of the Giant players probably were not the sons and grandsons of major league ball players. I said nothing of this fact because I knew that, however fantastic the desire to be a poet seemed, the desire to be a ball player would have inspired far greater scorn and ridicule. Nevertheless the family's attitude made me silent about poetry and being a poet for several years. I felt enough self-doubt within myself and did not want to have to be exposed to the doubt of other human beings.

Adults and my peers on the block and at school also were opposed, in a variety of ways, to the fact that I was a devout reader and patron of the neighborhood branch of the public library. The adults thought that a great deal of reading was not good for the health of a growing boy; the boys on the block, however, felt that it was a pretentious affectation, a transparent way of showing off and making believe that I was learned. One boy who was just as passionate and fanatical about the standing of the Giants as I was told me that it was impossible for one to be both a Giant rooter and an ardent reader of books. Since I knew very well that I was devoted to reading and to the Giants, my peer's incredulity seemed very strange to me, but left me untroubled. It struck me as equally strange that everyone, adults as well as children, was not as delighted by both books and baseball, but seemed preoccupied with matters which were comparatively trivial or quite unexciting.

A good many other incidents of the same kind made the lot of a growing highbrow and baseball fan full of doubt and fear. But nothing and no one had ever seemed as absolute in making all hope and ambition seem delusion and doomed as

Spengler. For no one had ever cited the very nature of history, past, present, and future, as a reason for fear and dread. As the school year continued and Christmas came near, the very nature of the weather—the cold, the slush, the icy pavement on which I walked to and from school—came to seem Spenglerian: The year was declining, just as Spengler said, whether or not anyone was pleased by the inexorable laws of nature and of history and of Spengler. By Christmas I was in a state of monotonous discouragement, partly because the more I learned of history, the more I encountered what seemed to be detailed confirmations of Spengler's description of all history. Athens had fallen, Rome had fallen, every empire, however strong, had fallen, sooner or later, and it was only the previous summer that the Giants had fallen into the second division long before the end of the pennant race.

The gloom of winter and history became so black that I ventured with the utmost timidity and shyness to ask the history teacher, at the end of one class, what he thought of Oswald Spengler's *The Decline of the West*. The bell had just rung and the other students were departing in haste and the teacher himself seemed eager to go elsewhere and skeptical. He may have thought an adult had suggested the question, for he saw how very embarrassed I was about asking it, and how eager at the same time. At any rate, he cut short his response of incredulity—"Don't tell me you've been reading Spengler!"—and said, with much kindness, that he himself never wasted his time on that kind of literary speculation, but that friends had told him that Spengler was systematic pessimism and extremely unscientific in character.

This dismissal of Spengler left me as full of perplexity as before I'd asked the question—I saw nothing wrong with being literary. I didn't know what systematic pessimism was, and Spengler seemed quite scientific to me, to judge by all his charts. I said nothing, but I must have looked disappointed, for the teacher then added that he had been told by a clever and intelligent friend that Spengler's learning was spurious; he had depended upon the eleventh edition of the *Encyclopedia Britannica* for much of his historical references, a kind of cheating which had been exposed when it was discovered that Spengler's historical errors in detail were very often identical with those in the eleventh *Britannica*.

It was impossible for me to believe that Spengler was dishonest and not really learned. The teacher grinned as he left, and it was only after sixteen years had passed that I found out he had been joking and what he had said was untrue: He had invented the canard, perhaps because he thought I ought not to be asking questions about authors like Spengler.

As I walked home from school that afternoon, I brooded about the history teacher's comment and explanation and felt that I was in a worse state of perplexity than I had been before forcing myself to question him: I had certainly wanted very much to be told that Spengler was wrong at least about the future, but it was inconceivable to me that so exalted a human being would stoop to dishonesty, the petty dishonesty of schoolboys, and use the *Encyclopedia Britannica* as a crib or pony, concealing the second-hand sources of his historical learning. Even at school few of us cheated in tests unless we were afraid of getting failing grades. And the same was true in games: It was no fun and no pride winning a punchball dishonestly. How then could it possibly be true that a man of Spengler's age and experience should be guilty of what schoolboys disdained except out of necessity? The more I thought about what the history teacher had said, the more insoluble the whole question became.

The Ego Is Always at the Wheel

On the one hand, it was impossible to think of Spengler as a dishonest author, all the more impossible because he was only seeking to establish unpleasant and unwelcome views which even he might not find agreeable and cheering. On the other hand, the history teacher, whatever his limitations, was certainly not the kind of person who accuses another man—and a famous one at that—of dishonesty when there is no justification at all for the accusation. I thought of other possible explanations and found them all equally mystifying: The one realm of possibility that I never examined at all was the true one, that the teacher was joking, something which should and would have occurred to me if, instead of being bemused and constrained by embarrassment and mostly unaware of whatever I was looking at, I had looked more attentively at the teacher's grin. By the end of the walk home I was exhausted and profoundly dissatisfied. I knew that I would never command sufficient courage to ask the history teacher the same question again, although I wished he would explain his explanations, and although, painfully enough, I might ask my next history teacher the same question when the new term began in February, that was more than a month in the future, which is to say, a very long time to wait and be impatient and gnawed by perplexity.

During the Christmas recess, the unanswered question made me go downtown on the Fifth Avenue Bus to the Public Library, to see if I were able to find reviews and other judgements of Spengler's work and perhaps his character as well. I had never before gone to the library at 42nd Street and Fifth Avenue, and the excitement which had increased continually as the bus made its leisurely way downtown, lumbering and obese, abruptly terminated and became disappointment, chagrin, and shame: I was refused admission to the library itself because I was too young. The guard at the door seemed to be insulted, as if his status had been reduced by my appearance; I myself not only felt insulted, but guilty of a *faux pas* in public.

Everything went from worst to worst. I felt more and more discouraged, more and more helpless, extremely ignorant, and cut off from the most important sources of information, and born too late in a world too old. Spengler was right, and this was what I had feared all along. By New Year's Day the Spenglerian sky and piddling monotonous rain made the new year seem as hopeless and as bleak as my own present and future.

After Christmas recess I was too downhearted to care very much about school. I stopped walking to and from school. I caught cold, and by the week of final examinations, there was, in a way, a certain kind of consolation in supposing that Spengler was correct. If Western civilization was in a state of decline, it was natural enough that I too should be declining and falling. I failed in plane geometry, French, and biology, and this result appeared in public on a list pinned upon the bulletin board, which meant automatic expulsion from that particular senior high school, Townsend Harris, which was then a kind of Rapid Advance high school and preparatory school of City College: Students were able to get the normal four years of work completed in three. My decline and fall was more than public shame, public disgrace, for I now had to go to an ordinary high school, one much nearer home, where I would probably encounter the scorn and derision of the boys of the neighborhood and the boys I had known in junior high school, most of them one term ahead of me.

The Ego Is Always at the Wheel

I no longer cared whether or not Spengler was right about Western civilization. Whether he was right or he was wrong, I was a has-been, as sportswriters say.

The darkest, most desperate hour occurred then, just as it has since then, just before dawn. The Giants acquired Rogers Hornsby, who was not only the greatest hitter by far in the National League, but who had been the manager and second baseman of the St. Louis Cardinals the year before and had not only succeeded in winning the National League pennant but accomplished a feat which was even then coming to seem more and more difficult, that of defeating the New York Yankees in the World Series of 1926. I immediately looked forward to the Giants' return to glory, to winning four pennants in a row again, and to surpassing the Yankees again and again: In fact, I felt convinced of something about which the sportswriter merely speculated—that Hornsby, at the peak of his powers, would surely beat Babe Ruth's home run record. Ruth was also at the peak of his powers, and he was the one Yankee who made me regret being a Giant fan; nevertheless, Hornsby was not only a great batter, he also possessed a great baseball mind. He would make the most of the short fences at the right and left field foul lines at the Polo Grounds and hit a great many more home runs than Ruth had ever hit; for it was true that Ruth was the great home run hitter, but his batting average was far smaller than that of Hornsby, who had hit over .400 several times.

These joyous speculations about an abundant and triumphant future as a Giant fan proved quite untrue: The Giants did not win the pennant in 1927, the Yankees won the World Series in four straight games, much to my disgust, and Ruth broke the home run record he had previously set. But my ignorance of the future pennant race was exceeded only by the optimism I felt, an optimism which soon, and with less justification, extended to other levels of existence, one after another.

The senior high school which I began to go to in February had a baseball team, a literary review, and a daily newspaper which published poems. The boys of the neighborhood and of the junior high school appeared to be pleased to see me and to be unaware of the fact that I had suffered the shameful humiliation of flunking out of Townsend Harris, unless I insisted on discussing the topic, which bored them, or left them indifferent. They were far more interested in the acquisition of Rogers Hornsby and even the detestable Yankee fans conceded that he was a very great batter indeed. As my optimism grew, my interest in history, Spengler, the fate of Western civilization, and the future became intense once again. Soon after, I encountered the advertisement of a book which was said to be a complete demonstration that Spengler was wrong. The book was named *Sunrise in the West,* and I determined to secure a copy as soon as I could make the money.

Meanwhile I began to write poems which I intended to submit to the high school periodicals, sufficiently encouraged by the fact that another author had written a book which declared that Spengler was wrong and that the future might not be as black as I had dreaded. One of my classes now was a course in American history, beginning with the discovery of America and immediately suggesting the possibility that Spengler might be wrong.

(Years after, I discovered that a good many adult young men had been just as distressed and dismayed as I was by Spengler's view of history and the future, although not all of them felt quite as depressed as I.)

During late winter and early spring, I was in a state of

profound jubilation, expectation, and creative inspiration, writing poems and anticipating the coming National League pennant race by playing the entire Giant schedule on a game which was popular among boys then. It consisted of two concentric circles: By spinning the propeller-like spokes, the outcome of each pitched ball could be determined, whether it was a ball, a strike, a foul, or it was hit fairly. Then the spinning began again, and the place where the spoke stopped on the inner circle determined whether the ball was a single, double, triple, double play, fly out, grounder out, sacrifice fly, and two small spaces on the inner band were reserved for stolen bases, home runs, and errors. Although the results were at times weird in relationship to the actual National League at that time, it was possible to generate overwhelming excitement.

Like this imaginary pennant race, literary composition also was full of excitement, problems, expectations, and disappointments, but I never expected them to occur no matter how often they had occurred before. It was the same feeling and expectation which occurred during the actual Major League season before each game began: I always expected the Giants to win, although I knew in an abstract sense that they never would win every game and no team ever had. The anticipation of victory before each game was great, and I was always astonished and painfully disappointed whenever they lost. In an emotional sense, it was as if I had excluded the possibility of loss before each game.

The painfulness of actuality far exceeded the disappointments I suffered when the Giants lost an imaginary game or when a new poem seemed very poor. It was possible to cope with the painfulness of an imaginary Giant defeat by immediately playing the next scheduled game. And it was often just as easy to begin a new poem. Then, as for years to come, the writing of a poem was either easy or impossible.

During the actual baseball season, however, one had to wait at least until the next day and very often until the following year before being able to resume the uninterrupted attitude of unqualified hope and indomitable optimism. It was still simpler to avoid the actuality and difficulty and painfulness of reality when I wrote poems. I resorted to the well-known and time-honored device of being my only reader.

When, a year and a half later, my poems were accepted and published by the high school paper and literary review, the results were very strange in a way which has a complicated bearing upon me during the year in which I strove with Spengler's philosophy of history. Other students were much impressed by the appearance of my poems in print, although most of them explicitly disliked poetry in all forms and were scornful of all the poets taught in English classes. Several teachers, who had regarded me as peculiar, viewed my poems as original, and only two readers, apparently, found nothing to admire in my poems and nothing exciting about my appearance in print: One was the relative who had been certain that I would never be able to write poems because my forebears had not been poets; the other unimpressed reader was myself.

The reasons for my disappointment were for the most part literary—I had begun to read poets who were far superior to those who formerly had been my models or influences. But the dismay I felt when I saw my poems in print was complicated by an attitude which comprehended a good deal more than standards of poetic style. I had expected to be overwhelmed by excitement, pride, and delight, and I also expected to be the object of mockery, not admiration on the part of other students, at least those who made their detestation of poetry clear again and again in English classes. The admiration and approval of some of the other students was all the more amazing and demoralizing because some of my admirers had not troubled to read the poems at all: They were simply pleased that they had appeared in print and they assumed that if they appeared in print, they must be good poems. I was pleased by their pleasure but it left me entirely unimpressed: How could an admiration which had nothing to do with reading the poems be regarded as anything but pointless, particularly when it had to be compared with my own feelings of severe disappointment, which made the admiration of others seem the result of ignorance to such an extent that I spoke to some of how poor the poems seemed to me and embarrassed and perplexed those to whom I did not seem very modest or very intent upon a conspicuous modesty.

Long before this strange and astonishing disappointment occurred, I was astounded and disappointed painfully when the Giants did not win the National Pennant race of 1927, which had seemed so assured and joyful a future reality to me when Rogers Hornsby was acquired during the previous winter. Then, as now, reality was very often astonishing and unpredictable: Sometimes the astonishment and unexpectedness of reality was pleasant and desirable, sometimes it was painful, unpleasant, or heartbreaking. It is now years since I first became aware that the reality of the future was very likely to be very different than any present image or expectation: Yet this awareness, recognition, or knowledge are likely to be astonishing and unpredictable in many ways so essentially the same as they were so long ago that I must make an admission which may be a confession: Experience has taught me nothing.

FUN WITH THE FAMOUS, STUNNED BY THE STARS

Fame corrupts, absolute fame corrupts absolutely, all great men are insane.

It has been my good fortune to meet great men now and then, and these encounters have been very rewarding, so I would like to crash the gate of posterity by hitching my wagon to these stars even if I have to mix metaphors and expose the extent to which I suffer from hero worship.

One of these great men was a celebrated metaphysician who told me that he was always very polite to other great metaphysicians in print, but did not really think they were very bright because if he did, he would have to stop thinking well of his own system of philosophy, which was not theirs. He chortled when he said this, and this habit is, I think, characteristic of great men: They tend to chortle.

Another great man was a famous poet and the first time I met him, he was visiting a mutual friend and his wife, and he had a new dog, and he was making unkind remarks about editors and critics. This caused an awkward silence because several of the critics were friends of his host and his host was a very kind man who did not like to think ill of anyone. This famous poet kept us all up until four o'clock in the morning with his cynical and dismaying stories, but what's the use of being a great poet if you can't do as you please and stay up late? The second time I met this truly great author was at a cocktail party for a poet who was not very good, not yet, anyway. The great author was standing nervously to one side, and looking as he felt: Neglected. I went to talk to him with the lady friend who had come with me, and he said that he had just written a new poem, but he was afraid to recite it to me because of the female element in his audience. She assured him she would not be offended, and she had in fact read everything from Aristophanes and Boccaccio to Henry Miller, John O'Hara, and that unjustly suppressed example of eighteenth-century prose, *The Memoirs of Fanny Hill.* So the great poet recited his new poem, smirking:

> *Mary had a little lamb,*
> *His name was Jesus Christ,*
> *God, not Joseph, was her ram,*
> *But Joseph took it nicet.*

We listeners were offended, not by the reference to sexual intercourse but by the lack of religious understanding and the appalling rhyme.

This disturbed our celebrity who thought that we had reasons which were not literary nor theological for being nervous and distressed. He spoke then of the poet for whom this cocktail party was being given and who was standing about four feet away.

"Do you think he is any good?" said the great poet. "I can't stand his work, but he sends it to me for criticism all the time."

I murmured back in a low voice, alarmed that the subject under discussion might overhear this opinion of his gifts.

"I ought not to go to these parties," said the great poet, "I talk too much."

We said something senseless in reply. Then another poet came to greet the great one and the two exchanged greetings which would have pleased Machiavelli, Metternich, and Richelieu. They both explained that they had not read any of the other's works for the past ten years, but had heard other people whom they respected very much speak with no little admiration about these works.

Then the other poet departed to get a new martini and left us to the mercy of the great poet again.

"What happened to that fellow?" the great poet asked me. "He used to be very gifted and I thought he would turn out well, but somehow he has just petered out. Do you think it was woman trouble? Or does he drink too much?"

I answered that I did not know much about him, fearful again that what was said would be overheard and feeling in all truth that I did not know anything much about anything anyhow.

This incident made me feel that to be a great poet was a mixed blessing at best, if that was the most serene, self-controlled, and Olympian one could be after many years of absolute success. And I also felt that I had better avoid these famous poets because they destroyed my literary illusions and social poise.

So when another famous poet, almost as famous as the previous one, said in a letter about other matters that he was going to be in town and hoped to meet me at last (the *at last* was because I had written to him and about him now and then for ten years) I was pleased but disturbed. I did not really want to meet him. I admired him too much, and was doing very well and did not want to take any unnecessary chances. So far as I was concerned, his work was sufficient for me by way of acquaintance.

First thing you know, I am going down the street and there is this great poet walking toward me. I recognized him by his photographs. He had arrived in town and he must have been on his way, I guess, to a luncheon engagement. Meanwhile I had planned to leave town that night for a hard-earned vacation, so I felt that I ought to say something to him, introduce myself, and explain that I was going out of town, but was very pleased to make his acquaintance.

As I thought of saying this, the great poet passed me. I turned and looked at him and decided to follow him and introduce myself to him as a matter of courtesy. But as I followed him, I wondered what I could possibly say to him? The first thing that came into my head was that I am very glad to meet you and your work has been deteriorating for the past fifteen years.

This did not seem the proper beginning and suggested that I had been warped by being forced to earn my living as a literary critic, but anyway I could not think of anything else to say to him.

Then it occurred to me that the right thing to do would be to ask him to my house for a drink. Before he arrived I would fortify myself with small talk, which I detest, and hard liquor, which I adore because it has often helped me to engage in small talk and relaxed persiflage, which I like very much.

I had heard that the great poet was on the wagon, but that was beside the point, I was the one who would do the social drinking.

Meanwhile the great poet seemed to have become aware that he was being followed, for he paused, stopped, looked at me as if to say what is all this about? I stopped too and made believe that I was waiting for someone. I was getting ready to speak to him politely and invite him to the house for a drink that afternoon when I remembered that the electric icebox had broken down, so there were no ice cubes.

That settled it. I turned about and went away and left the great poet in peace. It is perfectly true that I could have bought some ice, but at the moment what I needed was an excuse and that was the excuse I needed.

Since that time, I have reflected upon the nature of this strange encounter. The great poet in question was a very shy man and yet a very worldly one, and one who in addition to becoming a great poet had tried very hard all his life to be a good human being. Perhaps some sense of this goodness made me afraid to meet him, for though shy, I have not tried very hard to be good. But this is idle speculation, it is true, and several other theories come to mind, for example that my admiration for this author was so great that I could no more bear to converse with him than to look into the dazzling sun. Certainly he was not at all like the other great authors I had conversed with, four in number, and I had no reason to think that he had anything but a mildly friendly feeling toward me, though obviously he did not care whether he saw me or not, and anyway many other people were overjoyed to entertain him.

What then can the reason be? Or reasons? I was not brought up very well and subsequent events have not tended, for the most part, to make me at ease either with the great or even with those who are not great. Yet I do manage to survive various encounters without irreparable damage on either side, so maybe there was something special here.

This is one extreme. At the other extreme are my encounters with another great poet, a friend of the first great poet and an admirer of the second, and a wonderful man too; shy, original, idiosyncratic, eccentric but at the same time what we might call, very concentric; that is to say, a man who makes it a point of honor to do what is expected of him by other people. Be that as it may, and I am basing these remarks on scattered impressions, I never have any trouble in talking to him, except sometimes it is a question of getting in a word edgewise. But he is usually talking about me and my welfare, which is one reason that he does not like to be interrupted. One time, for example, he had just found out that my lordly salary was fifty-two dollars a week and he was very much upset to hear this, and he tried to explain to me how I could make a great deal more money doing hardly any work at all. But the story of our evenings deserves a special account, I think, and what I want to bring out here was that I had told him about what happened when I did not go up and say hello to the other great poet, and he was very interested, and he said that he would probably have felt and acted just as I did. The news depressed me, so I asked the waiter for a double martini (this great man drinks only gin and he does not like anyone else to drink anything else in his company and it was when he learned that I liked gin very much that he concluded that I had good taste and knew how to live), and he asked for a double martini too, and before long we were reciting to each other just like a barber shop quartet:

> 'In the beginning was the word,'
> Superfetation of τὸ ἕν—

"Very witty, very witty," said my drinking companion, "perhaps one of the most brilliant remarks about life, love, language, and the Incarnation that has ever been uttered."

It was time for him to go to Grand Central Station, so we started out, chanting in antiphony to the disregard of one and all.

"Poetry is like electric light," I remarked as he went through the gates, "good at night, dismal in the daytime. Truly we are fortunate."

"Stick to gin and regular meters," he cried to me as he gave the redcap his suitcases and walked away, resembling Jupiter on his way home to Juno.

"Give me enough hope and I'll hang myself," I said by way of farewell.

BOOKS BY DELMORE SCHWARTZ

The Ego Is Always at the Wheel: Bagatelles. Edited by Robert Phillips. New Directions, 1986.

Portrait of Delmore: The Journals and Notes of Delmore Schwartz, 1939–1959. Edited by Elizabeth Pollet. Farrar, Straus & Giroux, 1986.

Letters of Delmore Schwartz. Edited by Robert Phillips. Ontario Review Press, 1984.

"I Am Cherry Alive," the Little Girl Sang. Harper & Row, 1979.

Last and Lost Poems. Edited by Robert Phillips. Vanguard Press, 1979.

In Dreams Begin Responsibilities: Eight Stories. New, revised edition. Edited by James Atlas. New Directions, 1978.

What Is To Be Given: Selected Poems. Edited by Douglas Dunn. Carcanet, 1976.

Selected Essays of Delmore Schwartz. Edited by Donald A. Dike and David H. Zucker. University of Chicago Press, 1970; 1986.

Selected Poems (1938–1958): Summer Knowledge. Reprint. New Directions, 1967.

Syracuse Poems 1964. Selected with a foreword by Delmore Schwartz. Syracuse University Press, 1965.

Successful Love and Other Stories. Corinth Books, 1961; Persea Books, 1986.

Summer Knowledge: New and Selected Poems. Doubleday & Co., 1959.

Vaudeville for a Princess and Other Poems. New Directions, 1950.

The World Is a Wedding. Stories. New Directions, 1948.

Genesis: Book I. Poetry. New Directions, 1943.

Shenandoah. Verse play. New Directions, 1941.

A Season in Hell by Arthur Rimbaud. Translation. New Directions, 1939; revised, 1940.

In Dreams Begin Responsibilities. Poems and stories. New Directions, 1938.